CABIN SAFETY

CENGAGE

Cabin Safety

Park Ji Hyeon
Huh Jung Won

ISBN-13: 978-89-6218-493-8

Cengage Learning Korea Ltd.
14F YTN Newsquare 76 Sangamsan-ro
Mapo-gu Seoul 03926 Korea
Tel: (82) 2 330 7000
Fax: (82) 2 330 7001

Cengage Learning is a leading provider of customized learning solutions with office locations around the globe, including Singapore, the United Kingdom, Australia, Mexico, Brazil, and Japan.
Locate your local office at: **www.cengage.com**

Cengage Learning products are represented in Canada by Nelson Education, Ltd.

To learn more about Cengage Learning Solutions, visit **www.cengageasia.com**

Printed in Korea
Print Number: 01 Print Year: 2021

CABIN SAFETY

Park Ji Hyeon, Huh Jung Won

CENGAGE

Andover • Melbourne • Mexico City • Stamford, CT • Toronto • Hong Kong • New Delhi • Seoul • Singapore • Tokyo

박지현
부산대학교 관광컨벤션학과 박사과정 수료

전) 대한항공 객실사무장
대한항공 서비스/안전 교관
대한항공 대통령 전용기 승무원

현) 영산대학교 항공관광학과 부교수
한국관광레저학회 부회장
한국관광레저학회 학술위원장

허정원
이화여자대학교 영어영문학 학사
서강대학교 영어영문학 석사
Boston University 영어교육학 석사
부산대학교 영어영문학 박사 수료

현) 영산대학교 항공관광학과 부교수

Cabin Safety

초판 1쇄 인쇄 | 2021년 7월 15일
초판 1쇄 발행 | 2021년 7월 20일

지은이 | 박지현, 허정원
발행인 | 송성헌
발행처 | 센게이지러닝코리아㈜
등록번호 | 제313-2007-000074호(2007.3.19.)
주소 | 서울시 마포구 상암산로 76 YTN 뉴스퀘어 14층
전화 | 02) 330-7000
이메일 | asia.infokorea@cengage.com
홈페이지 | www.cengage.co.kr
ISBN : 978-89-6218-493-8

정가 23,000원

Preface

Cabin Safety is mainly for people who want to be a cabin crew. The cabin crew has various roles, but all tasks are carried out with a focus on safety. Safety work is the most important duty of the cabin crew. It goes beyond the safety demonstration before a flight, and it encompasses a range of different disciplines, topics, and processes, so it is hard to fully understand at first. We tried to make it easier for students to understand the contents by presenting various examples and to allow students to actively participate in class through practices and team discussions.

Cabin Safety has 4 parts.
Part 1 is Aircraft Overview. You will learn general information about aircraft so you can get used to the technical terms about aircraft and safety.
Part 2 is In-Flight Safety Regulation. In accordance with the real time working routines of flight attendants, you will learn the normal safety regulations that flight attendants must know.
Part 3 is Managing Emergency Situations. Responding to an emergency situation is one of the most important tasks of flight attendants. In this part, you will learn how to deal with common aircraft accidents such as cabin fire, decompression, and emergency evacuation.
Part 4 is Aviation Security. In this part, you will learn about aircraft security procedures, how to handle unruly passengers, and how to respond to bomb threats and hijacking situations. It is vital to learn how to deal with such security issues because they are directly related to the safety of passengers.

International Air Transport Association (IATA) is the trade association for the world's airlines and 290 airlines worldwide are enlisted as members. All IATA members should follow the guidelines of IATA to maintain membership. Therefore, the contents of this book are mainly based on the IATA's Airline Cabin Crew Training manual.
We hope those who study this book can widen the scope of understanding on cabin safety and security, and eventually achieve your goal, to be a flight attendant, that you eager for.

CONTENTS

PART 4 Aviation Security 171

PART 1

Aircraft Overview

Chapter

1

Aircraft in General

I. Aircraft Classification

An aircraft is a machine that is able to fly by gaining support from the air. Common examples of aircraft include airplanes, helicopters, airships (including blimps), gliders, and hot air balloons. In this book, aircraft is defined as jet engine airplane.

• **Examples of Aircraft**

Vytautas Kielaitis / Shutterstock.com

1. Aircraft Classification by Number of Aisles

Aircraft which are configured with one aisle are referred to as single aisle aircraft or **narrow body aircraft**. Aircraft with two aisles are called dual aisle aircraft or **wide body aircraft**.

1) Wide Body Aircraft

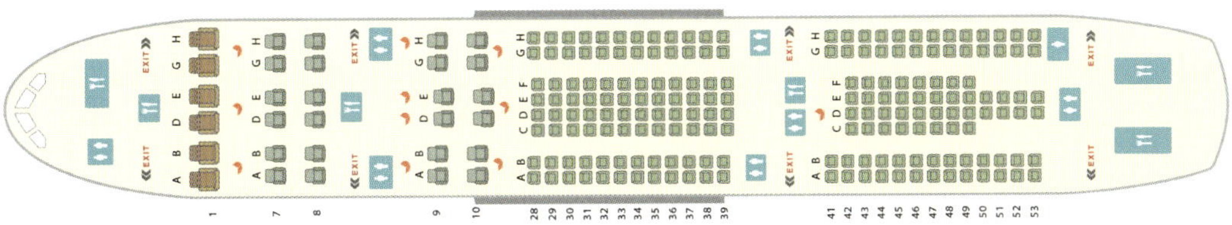

2) Narrow Body Aircraft

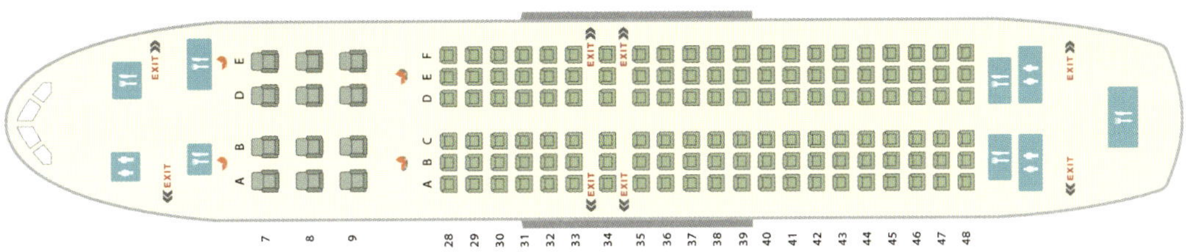

2. Aircraft Classification by Number of Engines

Aircraft have two, three, or four engines. Commercial aircraft normally have two or four engines. Due to fuel efficiency, airlines prefer two-engine aircraft.

- **Two Engine Aircraft**

Heather Dunbar / Shutterstock.com

- **Four Engine Aircraft**

Heather Dunbar / Shutterstock.com

3. Aircraft Classification by Manufacturer

Boeing, Airbus, Bombardier, Embraer are the globally known top 4 commercial aircraft manufacturers.

1) Boeing

Boeing is the largest manufacturer of commercial jetliners which is based in USA, and was established on July 15, 1916. Boeing's representative aircraft are B737, B747, and B777. (boeing.com)

2) Airbus

Airbus is one of the world's leading aircraft manufacturers. Airbus is based in Europe and was established on December 18, 1970. Airbus's representative aircraft are A320, A380, and A350. (airbus.com)

3) Bombardier

Bombardier is a global transportation company which operates two kinds of businesses: aerospace and rail transportation. In the aerospace category, Bombardier is the world's third largest civil aircraft manufacturer. Bombardier manufactured the CS series, which now Airbus has ownership of. (bombardier.com)

4) Embraer

Embraer is the Brazilian rival of Bombardier whose relationship is similar to the close competition between Airbus and Boeing. Embraer manufactures small jet-engine aircraft such as E-Jets and ERJ. (embraer.com)

II. Aircraft Type

1. Types of Boeing Aircraft

Boeing currently produces commercial aircraft such as 737max, 747-8, 767, 777, 777X, and 787.

• **737 Max**

Andreas Zeitler / Shutterstock.com

• **747-8**

Soos Jozsef / Shutterstock.com

• **767**

viper-zero / Shutterstock.com

• **777**

Jordan Tan / Shutterstock.com

• **777X**

Andrew Bondarchuk / Shutterstock.com

• **787**

vaalaa / Shutterstock.com

2. Types of Airbus Aircraft

Airbus currently produces commercial aircraft such as 320, 330, and 350 XWB.

• **A320**

Art Konovalov / Shutterstock.com

• **A350XWB**

vaalaa / Shutterstock.com

• **A380**

Ventura / Shutterstock.com

Question

What are the top 5 best-selling aircraft in commercial aviation history?

(Source: https://www.safran-group.com)

Ⅲ. Aircraft Dimensions

1. Length

'Length' refers to the distance from the nose to the end of the tail section of the aircraft.

2. Wingspan

'Wingspan' refers to the distance from tip of one wing to tip of the other wing of the aircraft.

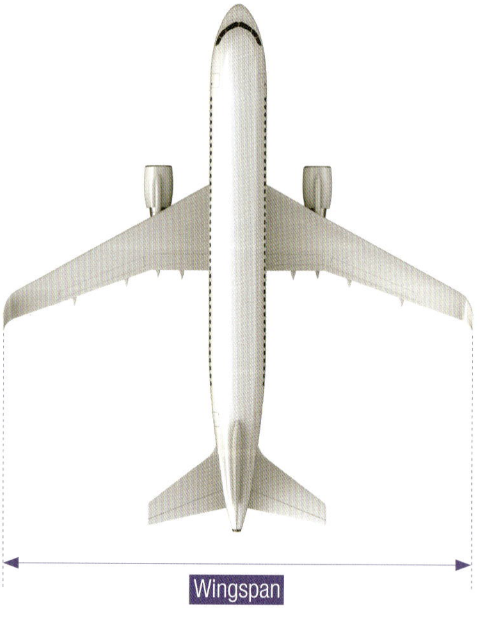

3. Height

'Height' refers to the distance from the ground to the top of the tail wing of the aircraft.

Ⅳ. Aircraft Capabilities

1. Maximum Operation Altitude

Altitude is the height of an aircraft that is flying above sea level. Maximum operation altitude refers to maximum altitude at which an aircraft can operate.

2. Normal Cruise Speed

Normal cruise speed is the rate an aircraft flies at maximum fuel efficiency for a sustained period.

3. Maximum Operation Range

Maximum operation range means the maximum operation distance an aircraft can fly while efficiently consuming its fuel.

• **B747-8**

Soos Jozsef / Shutterstock.com

Aircraft Capabilities

· **Maximum Operation Altitude :** 13,100m
· **Normal Cruise Speed :** 920km/hr
· **Maximum Operation Range :** 13,100km

Ⅴ. Aircraft Versions

Some aircraft types have more than one variation. These variations are called 'versions'.

Aircraft performance and size vary by versions. For example, Boeing 787 has three different versions which are 787-8, 787-9, and 787-10.

• B787-8

Market Opener

Acambium64 / Shutterstock.com

· Range : 13.620km
· Length : 56.69m
· Height : 17m
· Passengers : 242

• B787-9

More Seats, More Range

viper-zero / Shutterstock.com

· Range : 14,140km
· Length : 63m
· Height : 17m
· Passengers : 290

• B787-10

Larger Demand Markets

Rainier Ampongan / Shutterstock.com

· Range : 11,910km
· Length : 68.27m
· Height : 17m
· Passengers : 330

VI. Aircraft Registration Number

Every civil aircraft must be marked on its exterior by an alphanumeric string, indicating its country of registration and its unique serial number.

1. Code for Country of Registration

US	Korea	Japan	China	UK	France	Thailand	Malaysia
N	HL	JA	B	G	F	HS	9M

2. Registration Mark (South Korea)

Category	Engine No.	Registration Mark	Marking
Turbo Jet Engine Airplane	Single Engine	7100-7199	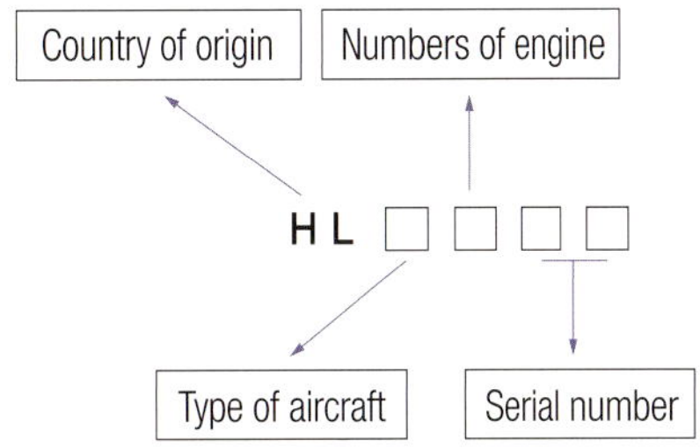
	Twin Engine	7200-7299	
		7500-7599	
		7700-7799	
		8200-8299	
	Triple Engine	7300-7399	
	Four Engine	7400-7499	
		7600-7699	
		8400-8499	* Only applicable to Korea
		8600-8699	

Alexander Gatsenko / Shutterstock.com

Craig Russell / Shutterstock.com

Vytautas Kielaitis / Shutterstock.com

Unknown Latitude Images / Shutterstock.com

Student Activity - **Team Discussion**

Read the article and answer the questions.

World's 5 longest flights

(Source: https://onemileatatime.com)

Q1. What are the five longest flights so far? Write down the flight route, flight distance, and the operating airline for each flight.

- 1st
- 2nd
- 3rd
- 4th
- 5th

Q2. What are the features of the aircraft which operates from Singapore to New York? (Refer to the Airbus homepage.)

- aircraft type
- version
- dimensions
- capability
- other features (seat availability, seat type, AVOD system and so on)

Q3. What are the features of the aircraft which operates from Auckland to Doha? (Refer to the Boeing homepage.)

- aircraft type
- version
- dimensions
- capability
- other features (seat availability, seat type, AVOD system and so on)

Q4. What are the features of the aircraft which operates from Perth to London? (Refer to the Boeing homepage.)

- aircraft type
- version
- dimensions
- capability
- other features (seat availability, seat type, AVOD system and so on)

Chapter

2

Aircraft Structure

I. Exterior Components

Aircraft are composed of fuselage, main wing, tail wing, engine, main landing gear, nose gear, and nose.

1. Fuselage

The fuselage is the main body of the aircraft. A passenger aircraft is divided into cockpit, cabin, and cargo area. A freighter is divided into cockpit and cargo. There are no windows on a freighter.

Eliyahu Yosef Parypa / Shutterstock.com

vaalaa / Shutterstock.com

2. Main Wing

ID1974 / Shutterstock.com

The main wings are attached to the middle of the fuselage. They regulate airflow that produces lift which enables an airplane to fly. Wings are also used as fuel tanks. There are flap, spoiler, aileron, and winglet in the main wing.

1) Flap

Flaps are used to maximize the lift and to help the airplane fly.

2) Spoiler

Spoilers are used to minimize the lift and to help aircraft stop.

3) Aileron

Ailerons are used in pairs to control the aircraft in rolling.

4) Winglet

Winglets are at the tips of the main wings to reduce drag by recovering of the tip vortex energy.

• B747 fuel tank can be filled up with 1086 drums.

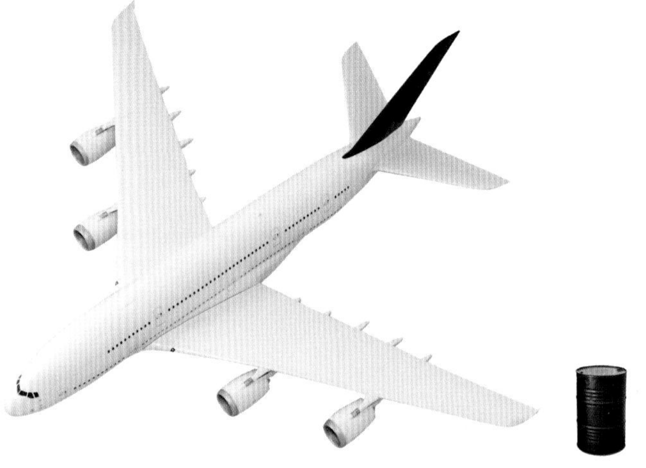

3. Tail Wing

The tail wing is composed of a vertical stabilizer and a horizontal stabilizer. The stabilizers have movable surfaces that assist in controlling the aircraft.

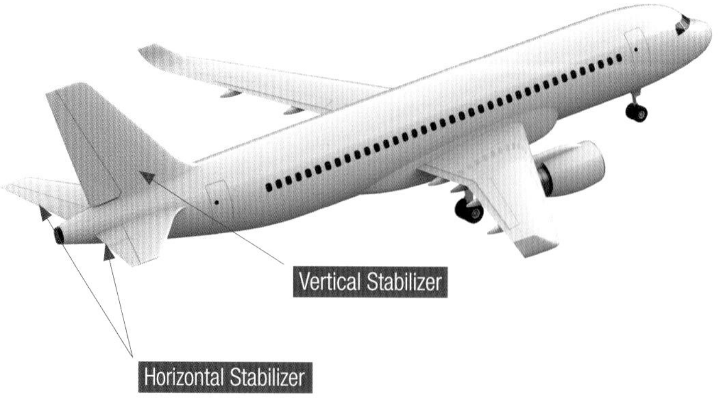

1) Rudder

A rudder is attached on the vertical stabilizer, and controls the aircraft in yawing.

2) Elevator

An elevator is attached on the horizontal stabilizer, and controls the aircraft in pitching.

Aircraft's Basic Movement

Aircraft have three basic movements: pitch, roll, and yaw.

Pitch is the movement of the aircraft as its nose moves up or down and is controlled by the elevators on the horizontal part of the tail section.

Roll occurs when one wingtip dips lower than the other and is controlled by the ailerons on the wings.

Yaw is the movement of the aircraft as its nose turns left or right and is controlled by the rudder on the tail.

4. Engine

Plane Photography / Shutterstock.com

The engine is the power source of aircraft. In general, aircraft engines are mounted on wings. Their numbers vary on aircraft types. Aircraft engines are numbered from left to right.

Four Forces Acting on an Aircraft During Flight

Weight is the natural force that tends to pull an aircraft to the earth when in flight.

Lift is the mechanical force that pushes an aircraft upward, against weight. Lift is generated by aircraft wings.

Drag is the force of air resistance.

Thrust is the force that moves the aircraft forward and is created by engines.

Phuong D. Nguyen / Shutterstock.com

5. Landing Gear

photomatika / Shutterstock.com

Landing gears are used on the ground. Landing gear in forward position is called nose gear. It mainly functions in balancing and controlling directions. Landing gears located in the middle of fuselage are the main landing gears and are mainly used for balancing, shock absorbing, and braking.

6. Nose

The Nose is located on the forward tip of the fuselage. The aircraft's radar system is positioned here.

Ⅱ. Interior Components

1. Cockpit

A flight crew controls the aircraft in the cockpit. It is composed of pilot seats, stowage areas, automated systems, emergency equipment, communication systems, a voice recorder (CVR: Cockpit Voice Recorder) and a flight data recorder (FDR: Flight Data Recorder) etc.

1) Pilot Seats

All seats in the cockpit have safety restraints. Cockpits are designed to be operated by either two or three pilots.

Fasttailwind / Shutterstock.com

2) Communication Systems

The pilots communicate with the cabin crew and passengers through an interphone system and a public address system.

(1) Interphone System

Allows two-way communication between the pilot and cabin crew.

(2) Public Address System

Allows one-way communication from the pilots to the cabin crew members and passengers.

(3) Cockpit to Ground Communication

Cockpit crews communicate with the ground through ACARS (Aircraft Communications Addressing & Reporting System) and SATCOM (Satellite Communication), company radio.

3) Black Box

A black box is an electronic device in an aircraft. There are two types of black box, which are a flight data recorder and cockpit voice recorder. Both black boxes are located in the tail section of the aircraft.

CVR (Cockpit Voice Recorder) records all cockpit conversations. It receives input from cockpit area microphone whenever power is applied to the aircraft. It continuously records and erases monitored conversation on 2 hours duration on solid state chip. **FDR (Flight Data Recorder)** records data such as altitude and airspeed.

4) Stowage Area

The stowage area, located behind the pilot seating area, is primarily for the pilots' luggage, coats, and hats. Some cockpits have a small closet and/or container with webbing to secure the articles.

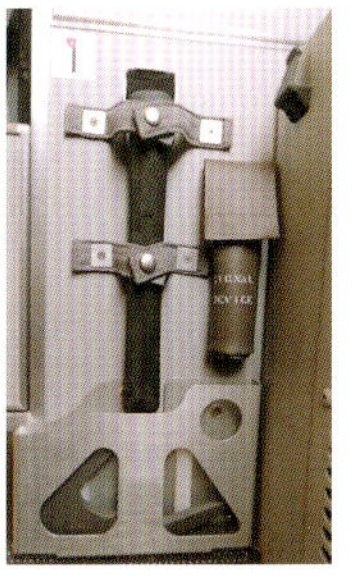

5) Emergency Equipment

The cockpit contains emergency equipment to be used in first aid, smoke and fire, and other emergency situations.

6) Reinforced Flight Deck Door

To maintain a secure cockpit environment, there is a door separating the cockpit from the cabin. After 9/11, airlines installed doors which has a locking mechanism controlled by switches inside the cockpit. This cockpit door is called a reinforced flight deck door, and it ensures the security of the cockpit from unauthorized personnel access. There are viewing hole and key pad on cockpit door.

2. Cabin

The cabin is located aft of the cockpit. It is the cabin crew's primary workplace. On a large aircraft, the cabin is divided into several areas called 'zones'.

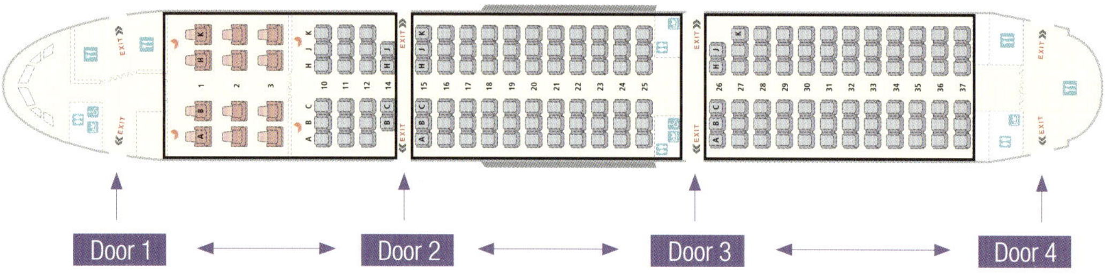

1) Components of Passenger Seat

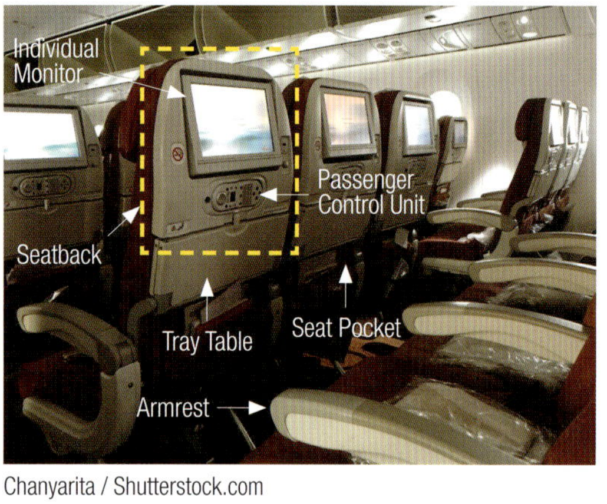

Chanyarita / Shutterstock.com

Maxene Huiyu / Shutterstock.com

(1) Footrest

A footrest is usually located under the seats in first class, business class, and premium economy class which is recently introduced in the aircraft.

(2) Tray Table

Most tray tables are located on the seatback. To use, lower the table from its stowed position. To stow, fold the table and secure with the twist lock. On some seats like a bulkhead seat, or a first class seat, the tray table is located inside the armrest.

(3) Armrest

The armrest has a control button to recline the seatback. On some aircraft, there is a PCU (Passenger Control Unit) to control in-flight entertainment, reading light, and attendant call.

(4) Seatback

The seat control button is located on the armrest for reclining purpose. Most seats can be reclined, except some emergency exit seats which block passengers' access to the emergency exit.

(5) Seat Pocket

Seat pockets containing the safety information card and in-flight magazine are on the back of each seat.

(6) PSU (Passenger Service Unit)

The PSU is located on the ceiling above each set of seats. PSU has 'No Smoking' sign, 'Fasten Seat Belt' sign, reading lights, passenger call button, and air ventilation.

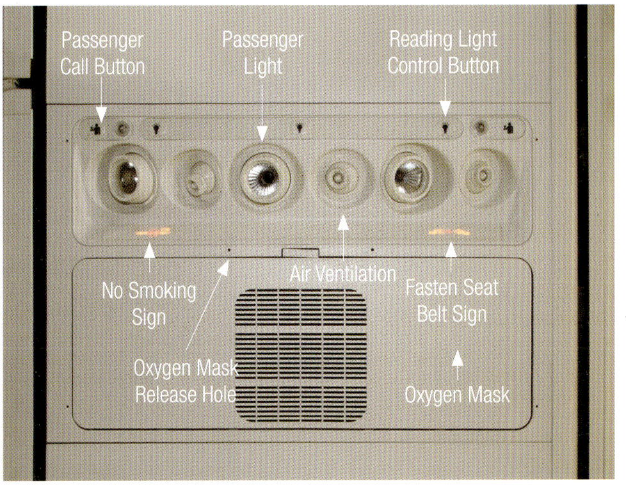

2) Jumpseat

Jumpseats are cabin crew's seats and they are located near the doors. There are single jumpseat and double jumpseats. Single jumpseat is occupied by 1 cabin crew. Double jumpseats are occupied by 2 cabin crew. Jumpseats are either forward-facing or aft-facing.

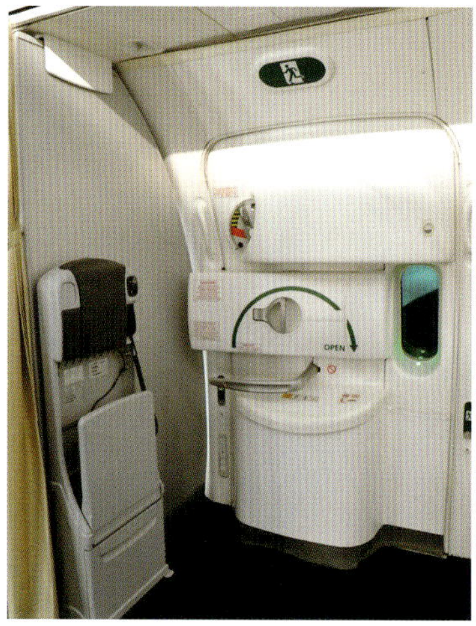

Jordan Tan / Shutterstock.com

3) Cabin Attendant Panel

There is a cabin attendant panel above or next to the jumpseats. Cabin crew can play boarding music and control the cabin light. Some panels also have a cabin temperature control button and emergency lighting switch.

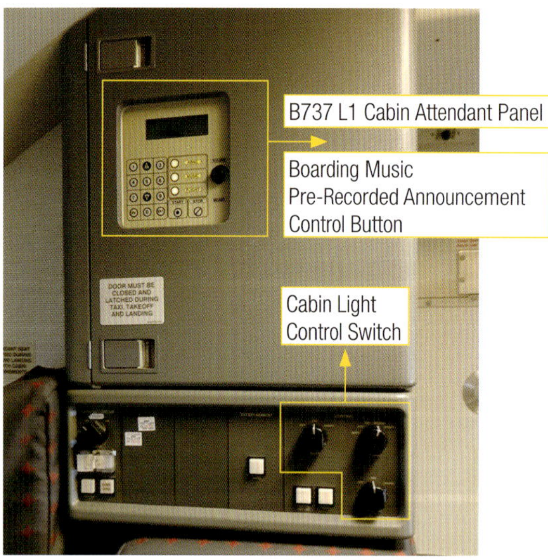

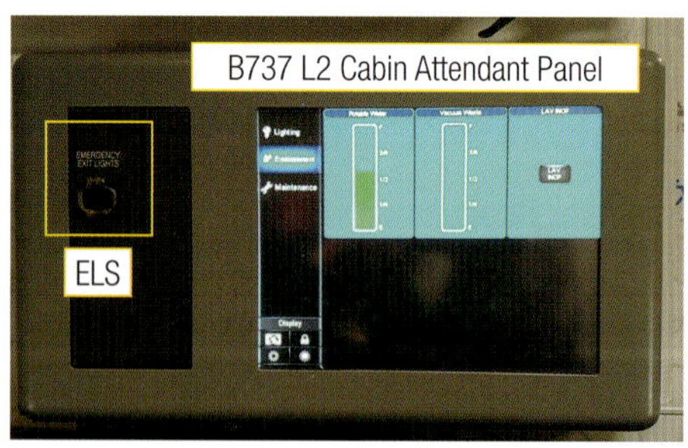

4) Emergency Equipment

Emergency equipment for first aid, smoke and fire, and other emergency situations are located throughout the cabin. Small emergency equipment picture placards are posted near each piece of equipment for easy access when needed.

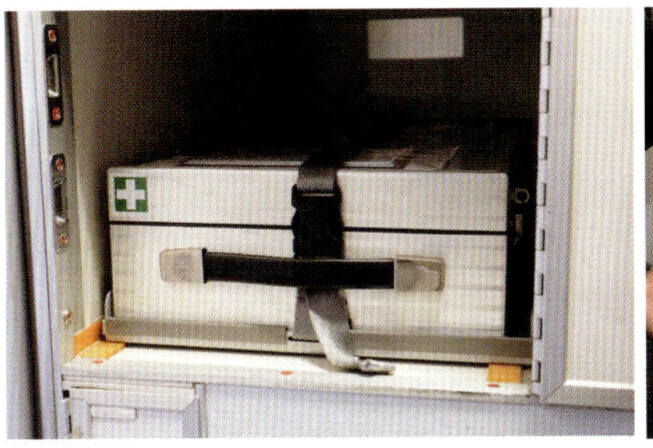 

5) Storage Area

(1) Overhead Bin

Overhead bins are located above the seats. They must be securely closed during any aircraft movement.

(2) Coatroom

Coatrooms are located throughout the cabin. They are for hanging items and can be used to accommodate odd sized or odd shaped baggage which do not fit in the overhead bins or under the seats.

(3) Under the Seat with the Seat Restraint Bar

A seat restraint bar is attached to the seat leg to restrain carry-on items placed under the seat. There are a forward and a side bar to secure items.

 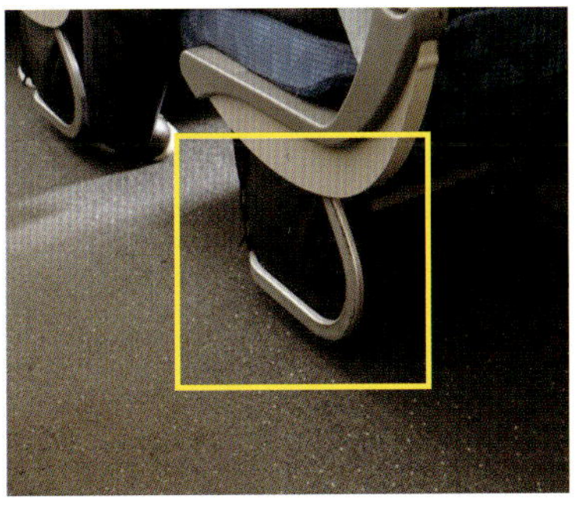 

NikomMaelao Production / Shutterstock.com

6) Galley

Food and beverage items are stowed and prepared in the galley. Galley locations vary according to aircraft type. They may be located forward, mid, and aft.

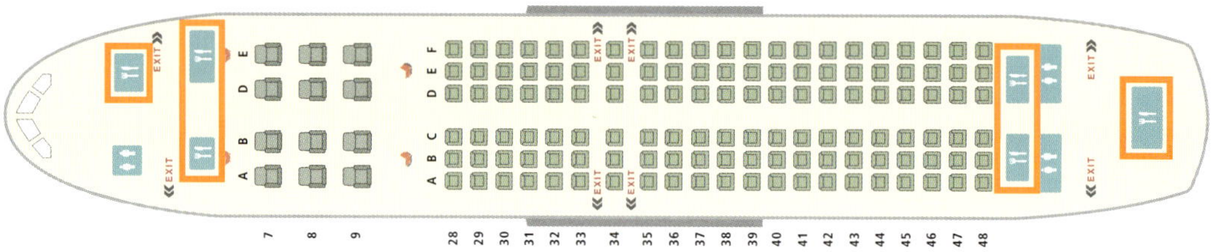

Jordan Tan / Shutterstock.com

(1) Oven

All ovens have racks, temperature controls, circuit breakers, and timers. Oven doors must be closed while the oven is running.

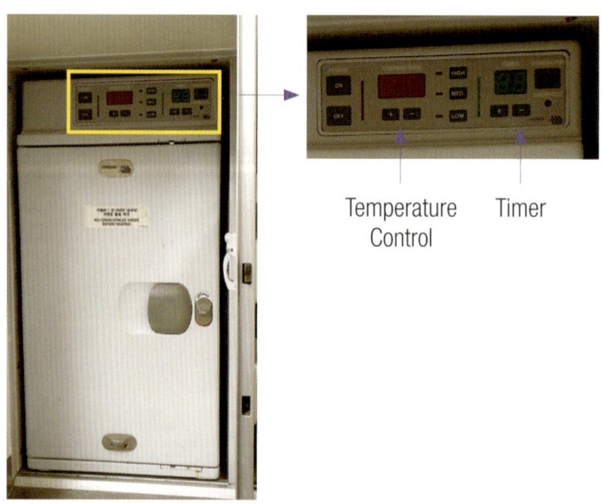

(2) Circuit Breakers

Electrical appliances like ovens and coffee makers have circuit breakers as safety measures. When a unit is overloaded, the corresponding circuit breaker pops out and cuts the power supply to the unit. Before resetting the circuit breaker, cabin crew should advise the captain. Resetting circuit breakers should not be allowed more than once.

• **Circuit Breakers**

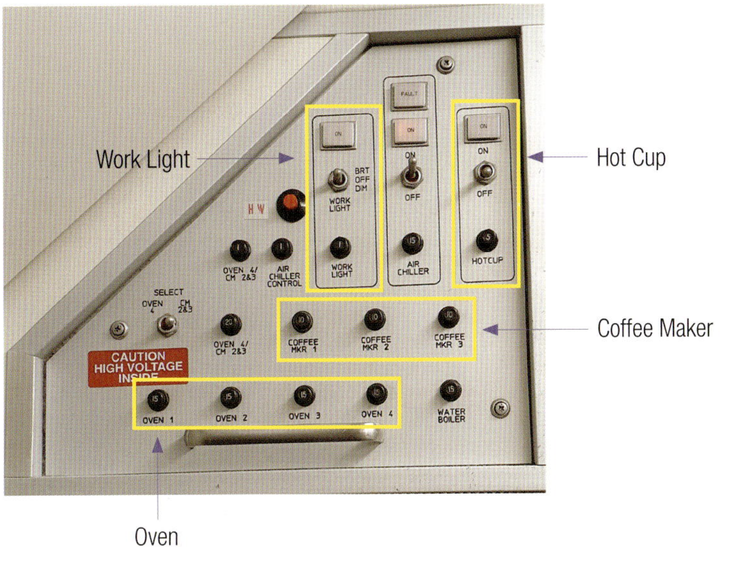

(3) Coffee Maker and Galley Water Shut-off Valve

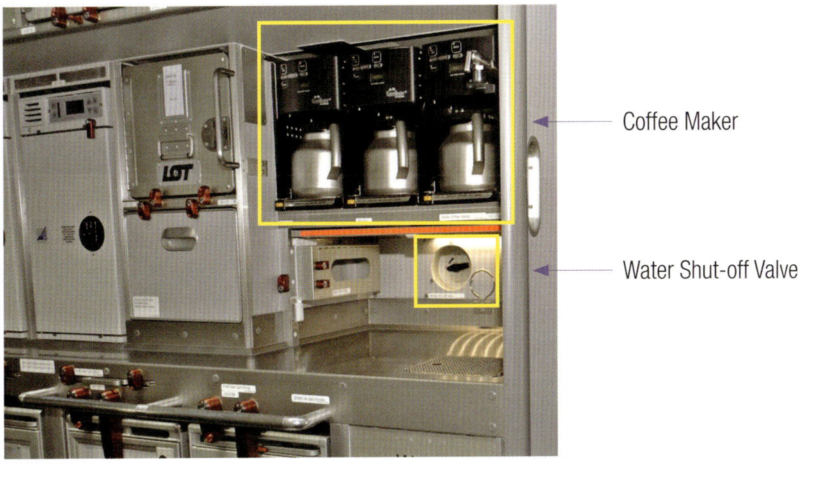

All galleys have coffee makers that include a warming pad, securing bar, and hot water faucet. And galley water shut-off valve is located near the water supply line. Valve location is placarded for easy access. To cut water supply, turn the handle to 'closed' or 'off' position.

(4) Drain and Water Faucet

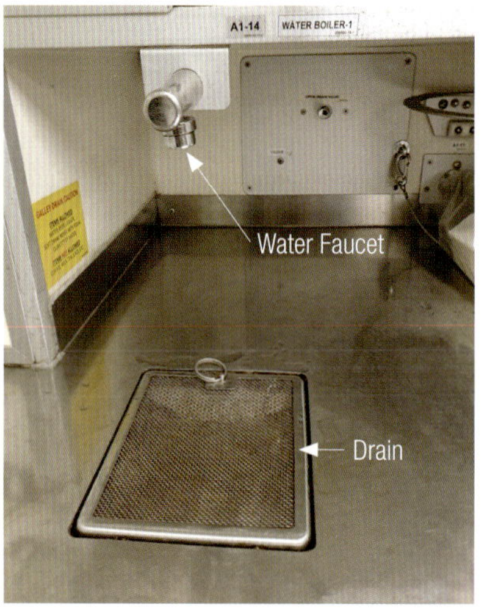

Each galley has a water faucet and drain. Since some drains empty outside the aircraft, never pour hot liquids in the drain while the aircraft is on the ground.

(5) Trash Receptacles

All galleys have built-in trash receptacles. Its cover should remain closed at all times.

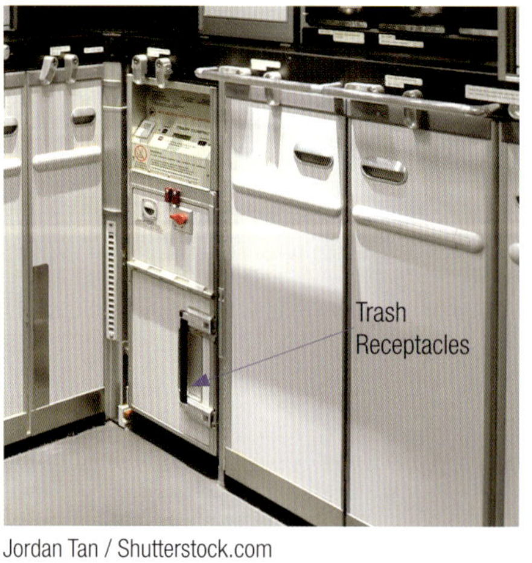

Jordan Tan / Shutterstock.com

(6) Stowage Compartments

All galleys have stowage compartments and drawers to store service items.

• **Compartment**

• **Drawer**

enchanted_fairy / Shutterstock.com

7) Lavatory

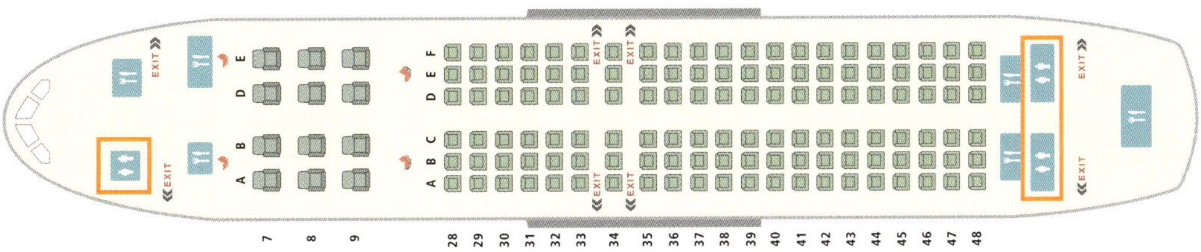

Lavatory locations and numbers vary on aircraft type. Inside the lavatory, there are a toilet facility, mirror, basin, a cabin crew call button, smoke detector, and 'Return to Seat' sign. The 'Return to Seat' sign is automatically illuminated when the 'Fasten Seat Belt' sign is turned on. Lavatory doors' locking system is connected to the lavatory lighting system, so when the door is locked the lavatory light is turned on. Locking the door also illuminates the 'Lavatory Occupied' sign in the cabin.

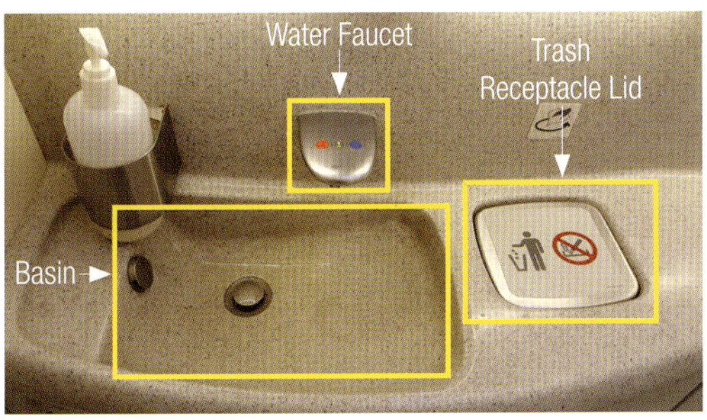

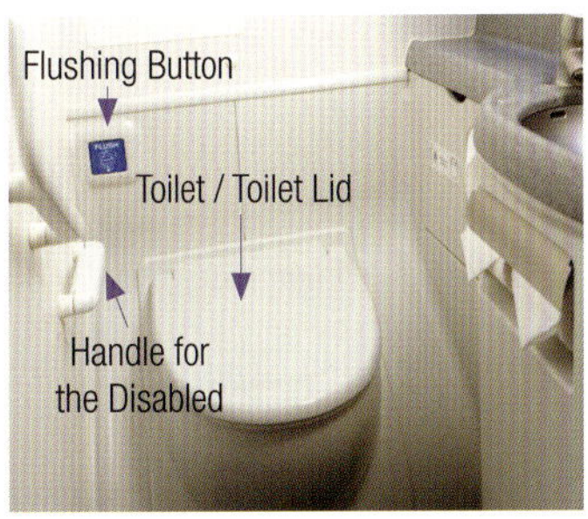

topimages / Shutterstock.com

topimages / Shutterstock.com

3. Cargo

Cargo is located underneath the cabin. It is used to store passengers' checked baggage and carry **live animals** and other cargo items. They are pressurized and some are climate-controlled. Cargo is loaded and unloaded a couple of different ways. On a larger aircraft, cargo is placed in containers called ULD (Unit Loading Device) and loaded into the cargo compartment, but most aircraft use belt loader to place cargo to the cargo compartment.

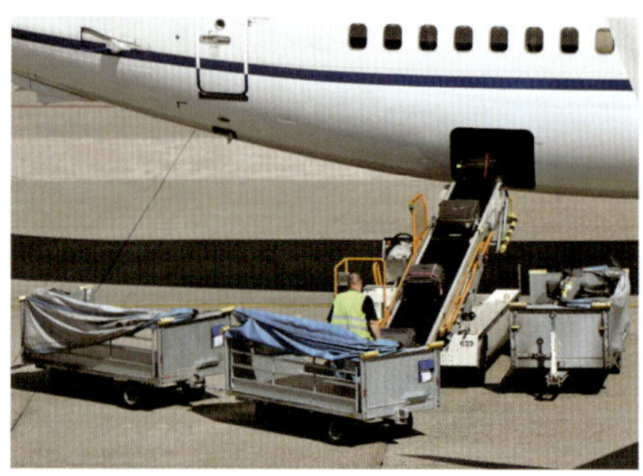
vaalaa / Shutterstock.com

Peter Gudella / Shutterstock.com

Student Activity - **Team Discussion**

Watch the video and answer the questions.

Airbus reinforced cockpit door description and procedure

(Source: https://youtu.be/ixEHV7c3VXs)

Q1. What are the features of the reinforced cockpit door?

Q2. Describe cockpit door normal access procedures.

Q3. When unauthorized personnel tried to open cockpit door, what action did cockpit crew take?

Q4. Describe cockpit door emergency access procedures.

Chapter

3

Aircraft System

There are power system, lighting system, communication system, entertainment system, water and waste system, environmental system and, oxygen system to operate the aircraft.

I. Power System

There are three kinds of power systems which are engine, APU, and GPU.

1. Engine

Engines supply electricity to run the other aircraft system and bleed air for air ventilation. They are attached to the wings of the fuselage or located at the rear of the fuselage. The number of engines is normally 2 or 4.

World's Top 4 Engine Manufacturers

GE Aviation

The General Electric GEnx is the fastest-selling, high-thrust jet engine in GE's aviation history with more than 1,600 engines on order. In addition to powering the four-engine Boeing 747-8, the GEnx engine is also the best-selling engine for the Boeing 787 Dreamliner. (geaviation.com)

Pratt & Whitney

Itsanan / Shutterstock.com

The Pratt & Whitney PW1000G engine powers five aircraft platforms, with the Airbus A320neo family, Bombardier C Series, and Embraer E-Jets E2 platforms already using them in commercial service. The GTF-powered A320neo has achieved a 16% reduction in fuel consumption, a 75% reduction in noise footprint, and a 50% reduction in nitrogen oxide emissions. (pw.utc.com)

Rolls-Royce

The Pearl 15 is the industry's most advanced business aviation engine, delivering greater power and efficiency for the Bombardier Global 5500 & 6500 aircraft and enabling top speeds of Mach 0.90. (rolls-royce.com)

Thor Jorgen Udvang / Shutterstock.com

CFM International

Safran (previously Snecma) and General Electric (GE) created a 50/50 joint company called CFM International to develop a commercial aircraft engine. The CFM56 is the world's best-selling aircraft engine, and powerplant of the best-selling Boeing 737 and Airbus A320 single-aisle jet families. A CFM56-powered aircraft is taking off somewhere in the world every 2 seconds - with these aircraft carrying over 7 million passengers a day. (cfmaeroengines.com)

2. Auxiliary Power Unit

The Auxiliary Power Unit (APU) is a small jet engine attached at the tail section of an aircraft. It supplies electrical power and bleed air for aircraft when the aircraft is on the ground. It is also used as an emergency back-up source and to start an engine.

3. Ground Power Unit

The Ground Power Unit (GPU) provides electricity and bleed air when the aircraft is on the ground.

Ⅱ. Lighting System

The aircraft is equipped with lights. The types of lights are cabin lights, passenger reading lights, lavatory lights, galley lights, cabin crew work lights and emergency lights.

1. Cabin Lights

The cabin lights are controlled by switches on the cabin attendant panel.

There are ceiling lights, side wall lights, window lights, and entry lights.

2. Passenger Reading Lights

The passenger reading light is above each of the passenger seats. Its control button is on the PSU (Passenger Service Unit) or PCU (Passenger Control Unit).

3. Lavatory Lights

The lavatory light is automatically turned on when the lavatory door is locked.

4. Galley Lights

The galley light control buttons are in the galley or in the cabin attendant panel. During the passenger rest period, galley lights are adjusted to dim.

5. Cabin Crew Work Lights

The cabin crew work light is above the jumpseats and its control button is at the jumpseat.

•Cabin

•Reading Light

•Lavatory Light

•Galley Light

•Cabin Crew Work Light

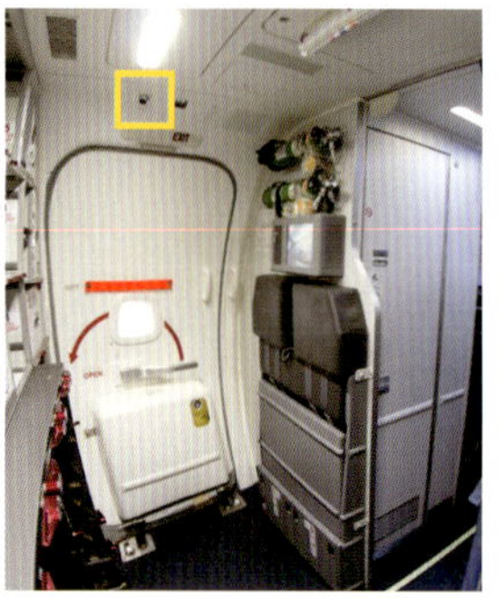

6. Emergency Lights

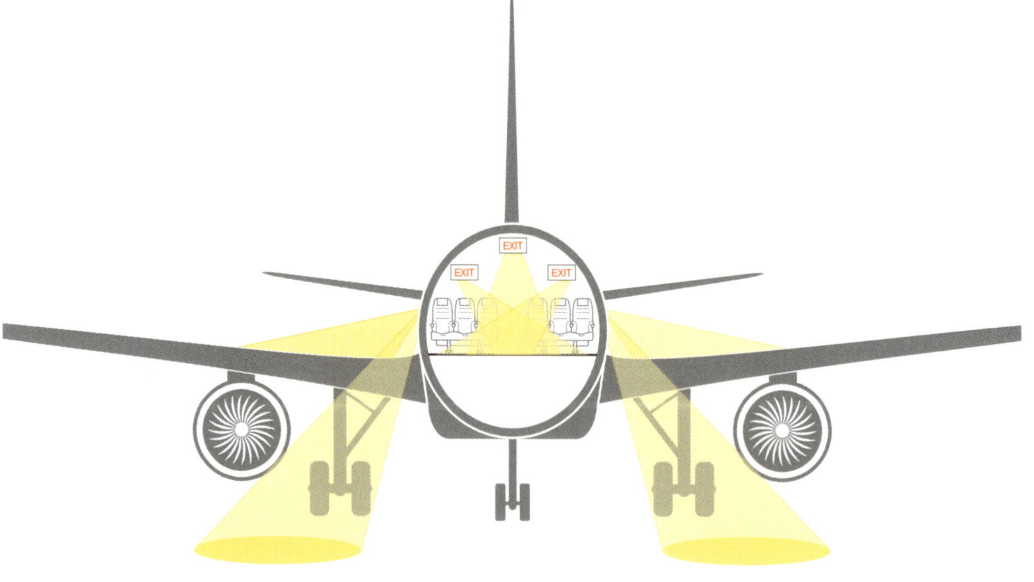

There are emergency lights for emergency.

They are activated automatically when there is a loss of electrical power or manually by the emergency light switch in the cockpit or in the cabin attendant panel. Emergency lights must include exit sign lights, interior cabin lights, escape path lights, and exterior emergency lights. Exterior emergency lights illuminate slides and other facilities on the outside of the aircraft. Emergency light must be battery powered and separate from main electrical power.

1) Location of Control Switch

- The emergency light switch (ELS) is located in the cockpit.
- The emergency light switch (ELS) is located in the cabin attendant panel.

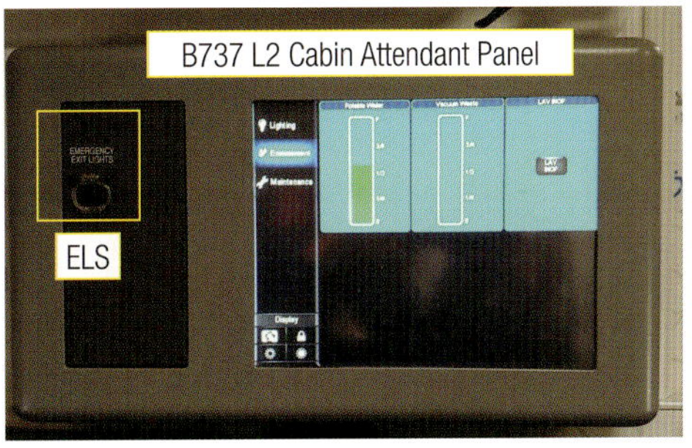

2) Activation of Emergency Lighting

Emergency lighting is activated:

- Automatically, by the loss of electrical power
- Manually, by the emergency light switch in the cockpit
- Manually, by the emergency light switch at the cabin attendant panel

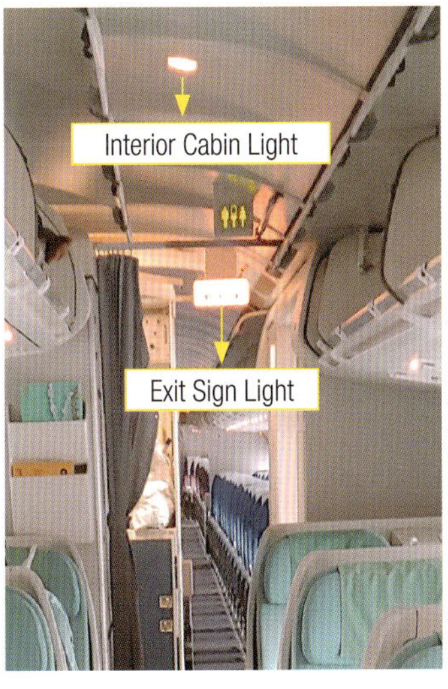

III. Communication System

The communication system includes the passenger call system, interphone system, public address system, passenger information sign.

1. Passenger Call System

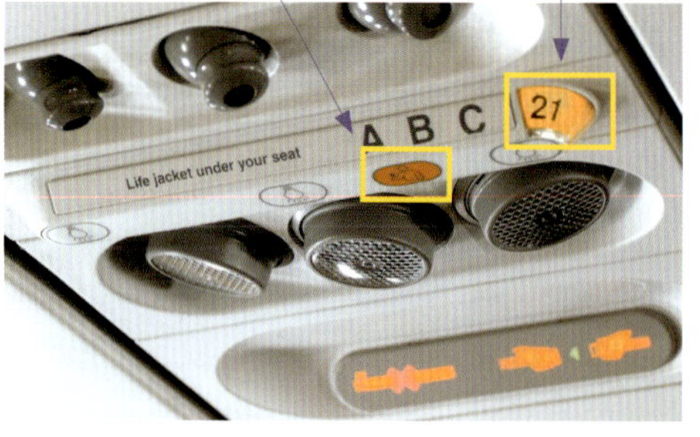

The passenger call system consists of a panel of lights and chime in the cabin. It is used when a passenger needs to communicate with a cabin crew. A cabin attendant call button is located at each passenger's seat either on the armrest or on the passenger service unit above the seat. There is also a call button in each lavatory. These calls can be noticed by the master call light display and chimes.

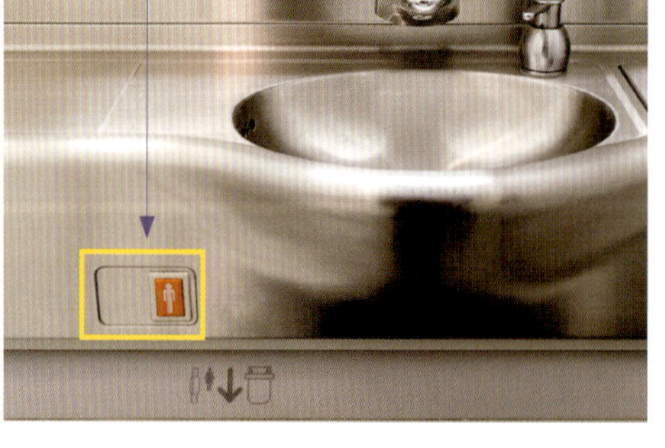

When a passenger presses the call button from his/her seat, a blue light comes on steady on the master call light display and, above the passenger seat, a light comes on to show the location and a single chime sounds in the cabin. When a passenger presses the call button in the lavatory, an amber light comes on steady on the master call light display, and a light on the outside wall of the lavatory comes on to show the location and a single chime sounds in the cabin.

Master Call Light Display

Master call light display is a device that indicates passenger call type and interphone call. It is on the ceiling above each zone, both on the left and the right side. There are three types of call light indicators in the master call light display, which are blue, amber, and red.

Blue: A passenger is calling from their seat.
Amber: The call is coming from the lavatory.
Red: The call is either from the cockpit or another cabin crew station.

2. Interphone System

The interphone system allows communication between cabins or between the cabin and the cockpit. To call from one cabin crew station to another, lift the handset from the holder and press the desired station. A red light illuminates on the master call light display and Hi/Lo chime sounds.

To answer the interphone call from other stations, take out the handset from the cradle and say your station and name. To reset the interphone system, return the handset to the holder or press the reset button.

3. Public Address System

The public address system is used to give an in-flight announcement. Handsets located at the jumpseat are used to make an in-flight announcement.

PA Priority

Cockpit station - Purser station (L1) - Other cabin attendant station - Prerecorded announcement - Video/Entertainment sound - Boarding music

Ko Aun Lee / Shutterstock.com

4. Passenger Information Sign

There are signs throughout the aircraft to convey information to both passengers and crew members.

1) Exit Sign

'Exit' signs are located in the vicinity of each window and door exit.

2) Fasten Seat Belt Sign

The 'Fasten Seat Belt' sign is located above passenger seats or near the bulkheads. When the 'Fasten Seat Belt' sign turns **on** or **off**, a single chime sounds.

3) No Smoking Sign

'No Smoking' signs are located above passenger seats, on bulkheads, and at the lavatories. When the 'No Smoking' sign turns **on** or **off** a single chime sounds.

4) Lavatory Occupied Sign

'Lavatory Occupied' signs are located on the ceiling panels in the cabin. The sign illuminates when cabin lavatories are in use.

IV. Entertainment System

Airlines provide various entertainments through the entertainment system for customer satisfaction.

1. Boarding Music

On all aircraft, boarding music is provided for passengers as they enter and leave the aircraft. The boarding music controls are located on the cabin attendant panel.

2. AVOD (Audio/Video On Demand)

10 years ago, it was difficult to find an aircraft that had individual monitor and video/audio on demand system. But, in recent years most aircraft are equipped with AVOD system. So, passengers can listen to music, watch movies, and even watch news on-air with their individual monitors.

World's Best In-flight Entertainment by Skytrack

Read the article and find out which airline is the winner for this year.

(Source: https://www.tripsavvy.com)

V. Water & Waste Systems

1. Water System

The aircraft needs fresh water for making coffee, drinking water and lavatory usage. There is a water tank in the belly. A water tank indicator is located at the attendant panel to indicate quantity of water. Water shut-off valves are available to shut off the water supply to the lavatory or galley area in case of flooding.

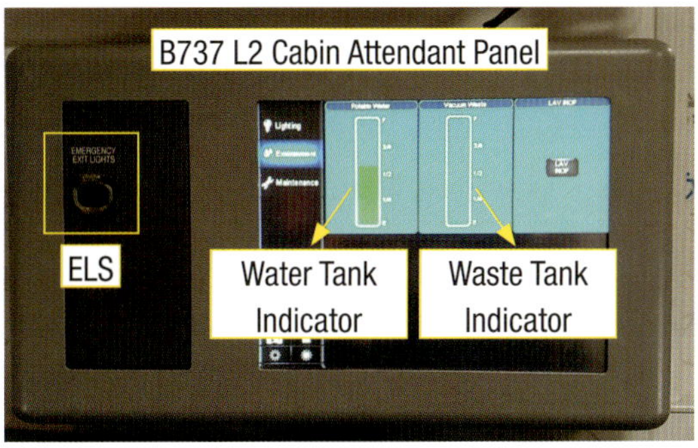

2. Waste System

There are lavatories in the cabin, so we need waste system that dispose of toilet waste. There is a waste tank. Toilet waste is sucked to the waste tank using the atmospheric pressure difference. The higher the altitude, the lower the external pressure compared to the internal pressure. So when you push the flushing button, waste system sucks waste of the toilet and sends it to a large waste tank at the bottom of the aircraft. After landing, lavatory truck connects the hose to the waste tank of the aircraft and finally disposes of it.

VI. Environmental Control System

There is a system to make the cabin environment comfortable to stay. The environmental control system (ECS) provides air, thermal control, and regulates the cabin air pressure.

1. Pressurization System

The pressurization system maintains cabin conditions similar to that at altitudes of between 5,000 feet and 8,000 feet. Altitude affects atmospheric pressure, temperature, and density of oxygen. With every 1,000 feet, the temperature drops by 2°C. If the ground temperature is 15°C, an altitude of 33,000 feet will be minus 50°C with very low pressure and oxygen. People would lose consciousness within 30 seconds. People can withstand pressures and air densities as high as 14,000 feet, but when aircraft flies above 14,000 feet, it must be pressurized to provide an adequate concentration of oxygen. For this reason, aircrafts are pressurized to simulate an altitude of 5,000 to 8,000 feet. This simulated altitude is called cabin altitude.

2. Air Ventilation System

Air from outside is sterilized at 200 °C by passing through the engine compressor before entering the cabin. The heated and compressed air then passes through an ozone purification system and an air conditioning system, and then is supplied to the cabin. The air is completely replaced every 2 - 3 minutes. As fresh air moves from top to bottom, any dust, odor, and carbon dioxide from passengers are also removed vertically and the air in the cabin is kept clean. Some aircraft have individual air vents and others have a centralized air ventilation system.

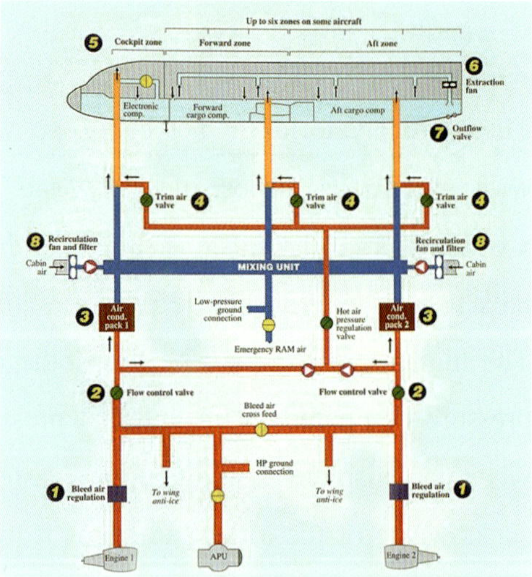

source: adapted from IATA Medical Report, June 2018

VII. Oxygen System

Aircraft are equipped with fixed oxygen systems to provide oxygen to passengers and crew members in the event of a decompression.

1. Decompression

Decompression is a loss of cabin pressure. Decompression may be caused by a leak in the seal around a door, a mechanical failure, a violent explosion, or a malfunctioning pressurization system. When decompression occurs, cabin altitude increases, and cabin pressure decreases, and oxygen density gets lower. There are two types of decompression, which are slow decompression and rapid decompression.

1) Types of Decompression

(1) Slow Decompression

Slow decompression is a slow loss of cabin pressure. It may be caused by a leak in the seal around the door or malfunctioning of pressurization system. When the slow decompression occurs, cabin altitude slowly rises, cabin pressure decreases, and oxygen density is slowly lowered. People feel discomfort in the ear and hear a whistling sound. Passengers and cabin crew can no longer breathe and lose their consciousness due to lack of oxygen.

(2) Rapid Decompression

Rapid decompression is a rapid loss of cabin pressure. It may be caused by metal fatigue or a bomb explosion. When the rapid decompression occurs, loud noise is caused, cabin temperature drops, sudden fogging is caused, and debris fly in the cabin.

©Getty Images Bank

2) Common Signs of Decompression

Whether it is slow or rapid, when the decompression occurs, three common phenomena occur:

- Oxygen masks drop.
- Decompression announcement automatically operates.
- 'No Smoking' sign and 'Fasten Seat Belt' sign are **on**.

2. Activation of Oxygen System

When cabin altitude reaches above 14,000 feet, oxygen masks will drop automatically. Oxygen compartments are located above each set of seats, above cabin crew jumpseats, in the lavatories and also in the cockpit. To make the oxygen flow, pull the mask down.

3. Types of Oxygen Systems

There are two types of oxygen systems which are chemically generated O_2 supply system and tank O_2 supply system.

1) Chemically-Generated O_2 Supply System

A chemical generator is located in each oxygen compartment and supplies oxygen to the mask in that compartment. To start, pull down a mask and then the chemical reaction produces oxygen. There is a slight delay before oxygen is produced. Oxygen is supplied for approximately 15 - 22 minutes. The chemical generator cannot be shut off once activated. The chemical reaction inside the generator produces intense heat and a strong burning odor.

2) Tank O_2 Supply System

If cabin altitude reaches approximately 14,000 feet, oxygen masks drop automatically. Each mask must be pulled down to allow oxygen to flow to that mask and the oxygen tank opens. Oxygen immediately flows from the tank to each oxygen compartment. Pulling any mask down towards you will pull the lanyard attached to a pin and open a valve. Oxygen will flow to the mask. Each mask must be pulled down to allow oxygen to flow to that mask. As the cabin altitude decreases back to normal, oxygen flow will decrease until the cabin altitude is about 10,000 feet. At this altitude, since oxygen is no longer needed, only a trace amount of oxygen will flow. A Tank O_2 Supply System can be shut off in the cockpit.

Student Activity - **Team Discussion**

Read the article and answer the questions.

Almost everyone in Southwest plane incident wore their oxygen mask incorrectly, flight attendant says

(Source: https://metro.co.uk)

Q1. What was the main cause of the decompression?

Q2. How should the passengers put on oxygen masks when oxygen masks drop during decompression?

Q3. How to activate the oxygen mask on B737?

Q4. Until when should passengers wear the oxygen mask?

Chapter

4

Aircraft Exits

There are three types of exits in the aircraft: door exit, overwing window exit, and cockpit window exit.

I. Door Exit

Sorbis / Shutterstock.com

Door exit is used as a doorway for passengers to get on board and deplane in normal situation and also used for evacuation in emergency situation. Door exits are evenly distributed throughout the aircraft and their locations and numbers vary on each aircraft.

1. Door Numbering

Doors are numbered from forward to backward and divided into left and right sides. The most forward door on the left side of the aircraft is denoted by **L1**. The most forward door on the right side of the aircraft is denoted by **R1**. The next door behind **L1** door is called **L2**. The same order of numbering continues.

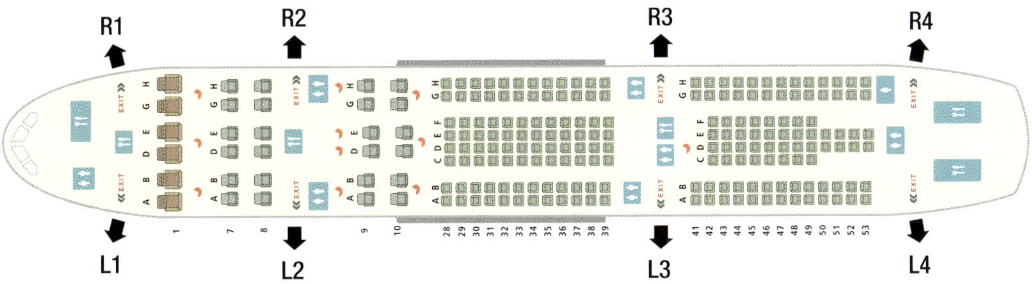

2. Components of Door Exit

1) A320

① **Door Locking Indicator:**
Used to indicate door locking status

② **Door Assist Handle & Assist Handle:**
Handles located on/or beside the door
Used to secure a crew member's safety when operating the door

③ **Door Operation Handle:**
Used to open/close the door

④ **Arming Lever:**
Used to engage or disengage the girt bar to the aircraft body

⑤ **Viewing Window:**
A small window to view inside/outside of the aircraft

⑥ **Slide Bustle:**
Protective case contains escape device

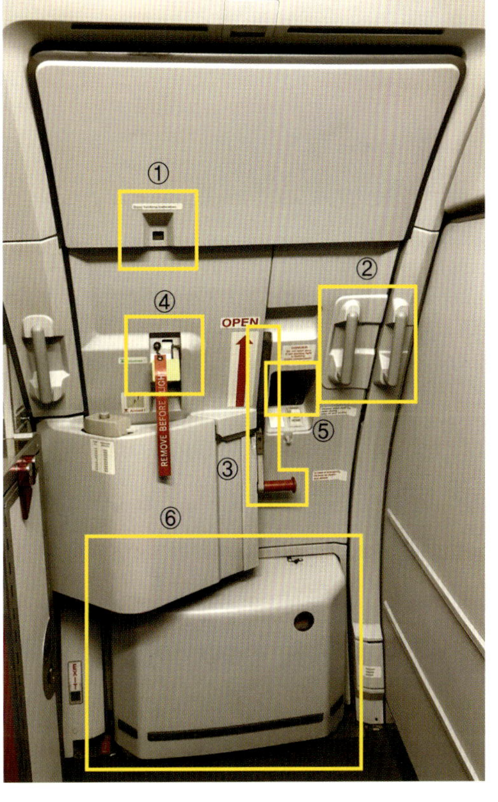

(1) Door Locking Indicator

Door locking indicator is installed on the upper side of the door to show whether door is fully closed or not. Red color means door is not completely closed, green color means door is fully closed. Not every aircraft door has the door locking indicators. B737 doesn't have door locking indicator. So, cabin crew should confirm the door locking status manually.

(2) Door Assist Handle & Assist Handle

Door assist handle and assist handle are handles located on/or beside the door and they secure cabin crew's safety. Since door is really heavy, cabin crew might fall down from the aircraft while opening and closing the door. For safety reasons, every time cabin crew open and close the door, they should hold the assist handle.

(3) Door Operation Handle

Door operation handle is used to open/close the door. Door can be opened when rotating or pulling the door operation handle.

(4) Arming Lever

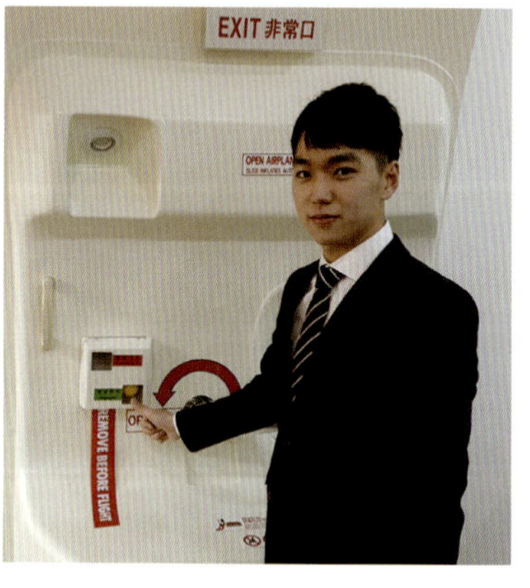

Arming lever is used to secure the girt bar to the fuselage. Girt bar is a metal stick. It is connected to the slide/raft and used to connect the slide/raft to the aircraft body.
If cabin crew change arming lever from the disarmed to the armed position, girt bar is secured to the fuselage. In the armed position, which means girt bar is secured to the aircraft body, if cabin crew open the door, slide/raft is inflated automatically.
According to aviation law, when passengers are on board, at least one floor-level exit must be available for normal or emergency exit. The term 'be available' means a door is in armed position or a step car is ready to use. Aircraft surface movement (push-back) is prohibited unless each door is armed for emergency exit. For surface movement, all exits must be armed and ready for evacuation.

(5) Viewing Window

Viewing window is a small window to view inside/outside. Cabin crew can check the outside condition through the viewing window. It is also used when cabin crew communicate with ground staff. For example, in case ground staff should open the door outside, cabin crew give thumb–up signal to ground staff to inform that door is ready to open.

(6) Slide Bustle

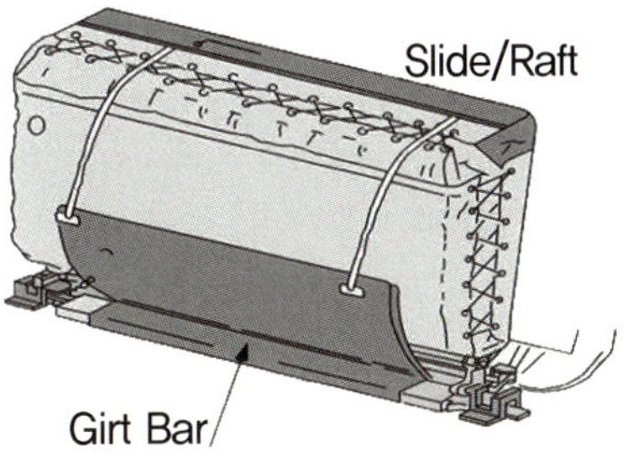

Protective case contains escape device.

There are two types of escape devices: slides and slide/rafts. Slides have a single lane and no side barriers. Slide/rafts have either single lane or dual lanes and have side barriers. In case of emergency landing on the water, slides can only be used as flotation devices, but slide/raft can be used as both flotation devices and life boats.

2) B737

① **Viewing Window:**
Used to assess the outside situation from the inside

② **Door Assist Handle and Assist Handle:**
Used to secure a crew member's safety when operating the door

③ **Door Operation Handle:**
Used to open and close the door

④ **Slide Bustle:**
Stores escape device

⑤ **Red Warning Flag:**
Used to indicate location of girt bar to prevent mis-inflation of escape device

⑥ **Girt Bar:**
Used to secure an escape device to the door sill of aircraft

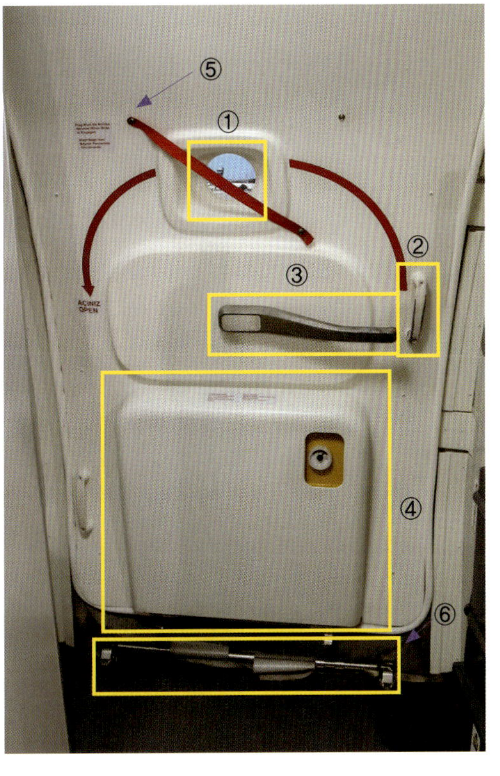

• **Disarmed (Girt Bar on Slide Bustle)**

A door must be disarmed not to deploy the slide and to open for regular boarding or deplaning. To disarm a door, the girt bar is engaged on the slide bustle and moves with the door.

• **Armed (Girt Bar to the Floor Fittings)**

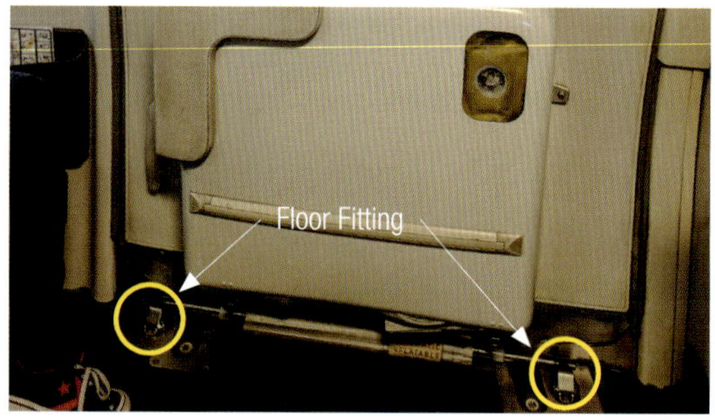

A door must be armed to deploy the slide in order to evacuate passengers after an emergency landing. To arm the door, the girt bar is connected to the aircraft floor fittings.

3. Components Which are Visible When Door is Opened

1) Gust Lock

A mechanism that keeps a hinged aircraft door in the **open** and **locked** position against the fuselage to prevent a gust of wind from closing the door.

2) Gust Lock Release Button/Handle/Lever

A mechanism that releases the gust lock so the door can be closed.

3) Safety Strap

Safety strap is not a safety device; it simply gives a warning to the cabin crew that the door is open. When neither stairs nor bridge is in place, place the safety strap across the open door.

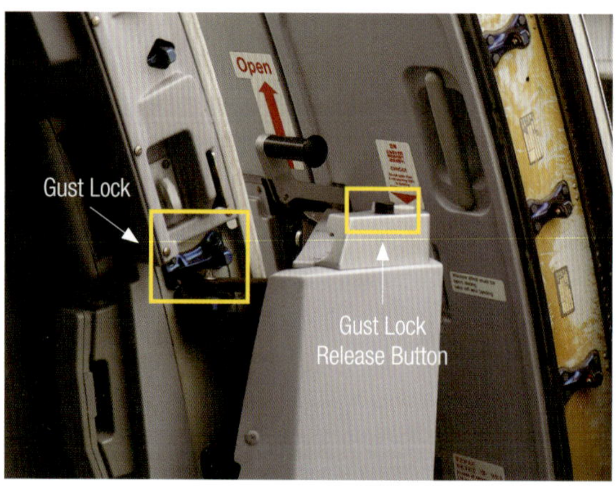

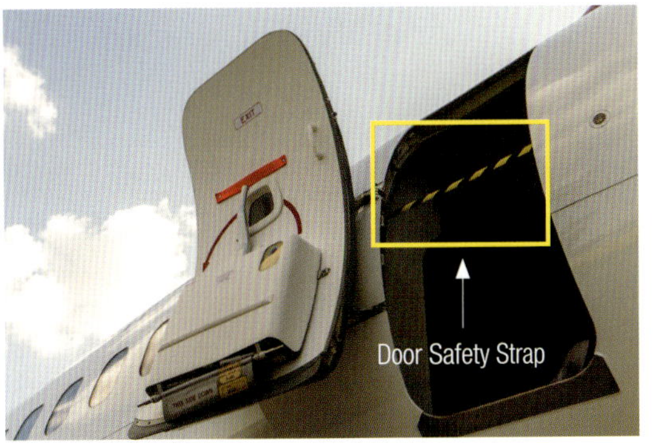

4. Operation of Door

1) To Open the Door in Normal Mode

- Check if 'Fasten Seat Belt' sign is off.
- Assess the outside condition.
- Check door mode is in disarmed/manual position.
- Open the door (Grab the assist handle using the door operation handle).
- Engage gust lock.

2) To Close the Door in Normal Mode

- Release gust lock.
- Hold assist handle and pull the door inward.
- Rotate/Pull down the door operating handle to close the door.
- Ensure the door is completely closed.

3) To Open the Door in Emergency Mode

- Assess the outside condition.
- Check if door mode is in armed/automatic position.
- Hold assist handle and open the door.
- Door opens automatically and gust locked to the fuselage.
- Pull the red manual inflation handle.

II. Overwing Window Exit

Some types of aircraft have removable window exits located over the wings, two on each side. These exits are used for escape in an emergency.

robert cicchetti / Shutterstock.com

1. Components

① **Operating Handle**

Used to open the overwing window exit

② **Window**

Used to assess the outside situation from inside

③ **Closing Strap**

Used when closing the door

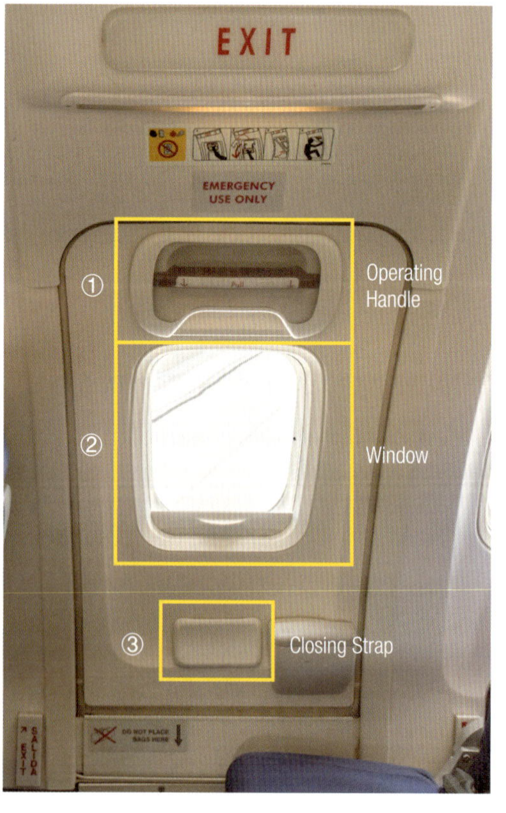

2. Overwing Window Exit Operation

Overwing window exit is used only in emergency. To open the overwing window exit,

- Assess the outside condition through the window.
- Grab the operating handle.
- Pull the operating handle downward and release.
- The exit will open outward and upward automatically and be fixed on the fuselage.

III. Cockpit Window Exit

Most cockpits have window exits. They are equipped with escape ropes leading to the ground.

First Class Photography / Shutterstock.com

First Class Photography / Shutterstock.com

Student Activity - **Team Discussion**

Read the article and answer the questions.

What happens when the emergency exit door opens mid-flight?

(Source: https://www.news.com.au)

Q1. Is it possible to open the door exit during mid-flight?

Q2. If not, why we cannot open the exit door?

Q3. If yes, what is going to happen then?

Student Activity - **Part I Review**

Q1. What is an aircraft?

Q2. Write what is described in each of the following.

A. The distance from nose to end of tail section (   )

B. The distance from tip of the one wing to tip of the other wing (   )

C. The distance from the ground to end of tail wing (   )

Q3. Write down three things that describe the capabilities of an aircraft.

Q4. What are the four forces acting on an aircraft?

Q5. Which of the following is true?

① Boeing, Airbus, Bombardier, GE are the global top 4 commercial aircraft manufacturers.

② Boeing currently produces commercial aircraft such as 737max, 747-8, 767, 777, 777X, 787.

③ Some type of aircraft have more than one variation. These variations are called 'type'.

④ A320 is the world's best-selling aircraft.

Student Activity - **Part I Review**

Q6. What are the components of the aircraft exterior?

Q7. Write the name of each part and explain the function.

ID1974 / Shutterstock.com

Q8. What are the components of the aircraft interior?

Q9. Fill in the blanks.

The cockpit is composed of ( ), stowage areas, ( ), emergency equipment, communication systems, ( ) and enhanced cockpit door.

Q10. Write the name of each part.

Q11. Where can passengers keep their luggage?

Q12. What is the following explanation about?

'This' is an electronic device in an aircraft which records all the information about its flight. When aircraft has crashed, people look into 'this', which is made up of a flight data recorder and cockpit voice recorder.

Q13. Fill in the blanks.

PA Priority

(   ) - Purser station (L1) - Other cabin attendant station - Prerecorded announcement - Video/Entertainment sound - (   )

Student Activity - **Part I Review**

Q14. What is the purpose of interphone system?

Q15. Fill in the blank.

( ) are activated automatically when there is a loss of electrical power or manually by the ELS in the cockpit or in the cabin attendant panel.

(Q16 - 19) Read the article and answer the questions.

Humans cannot survive long at the heights reached during flights, because the air is so thin, and so aircraft cabins are artificially maintained at a pressure similar to that encountered at 8,000 feet or less. (**16**)

This is achieved by taking air from one of the engines after it has been compressed by a series of fan blades prior to being ignited to provide forward thrust. This is known as (**17**).

Without artificially pressurized air, passengers and crew suffer a condition known as hypoxia, which can cause them to lose what is known as 'useful consciousness' within a few minutes (**18**).* So, the (**16**) reaches 14,000 feet, (**19**) are automatically drop.

Q16. What is 'this simulated altitude' called?

Q17. What is 'this compressed air'?

* Source: Gerry, B. (2018, July 14). Pilots and passengers have just minutes before decompression knocks them out. *The Irish Times*. Retrieved from https://www.irishtimes.com/

Q18. **Without artificially pressurized air, what is going to happen in the cabin?**

Q19. **Fill in the blank.**

Q20. **What is the purpose of the oxygen system ?**

Q21. **Write down the different types of exits.**

Q22. **What is housed in a slide bustle?**

Student Activity - **Part I Review**

Q23. **What is the explanation below?**

'This' is a metal stick to lock the escape device to the aircraft's floor.

Q24. **How do you call the third door on the right?**

Q25. **What does the explanation below describe?**

It is installed above the B737's wing and can be used as an emergency escape path.

Q26. **Write down the door normal operation procedures.**

PART

2

In-Flight Safety Regulation

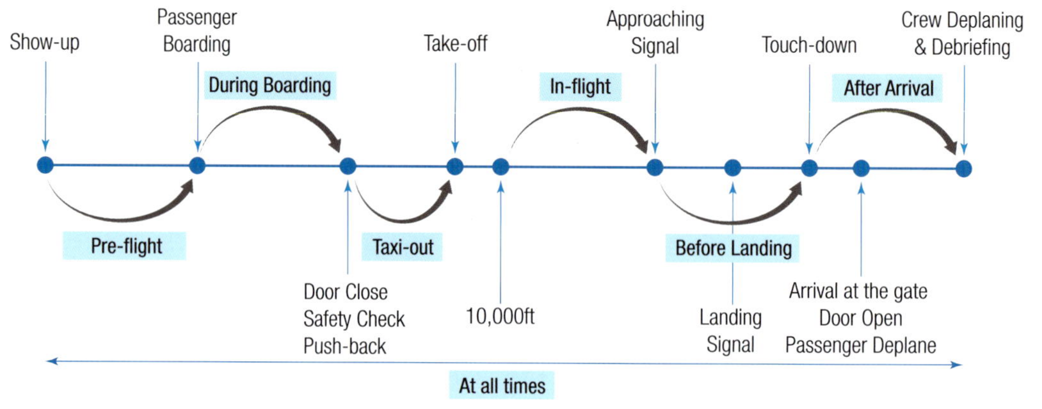

Regulations are rules that cabin crew must comply with when they are on duty. It is divided into several parts according to the stages of flight which are passenger boarding, push-back, take-off, approaching and landing signals, touch-down and arrival at the gate. To understand the in-flight safety regulation, cabin crew must know each stage of the flight.

From crew show-up to before passenger boarding, we call this period **pre-flight**. From passenger boarding to before push-back; **during boarding**, from push-back to right before take-off, **taxi-out;** from passing through 10,000ft to before approaching signal; **in-flight**. The period from approaching signal to before touch-down is called **before landing**, from touch-down to before arrival at the gate is **taxi-in** and from taxi-in to before crew deplane, is called **after arrival**.

In Part 2, you will study safety related regulations which cabin crew must know. Regulation is divided into several parts according to the stages of flights. From Chapter 5, we will look at the main regulations and guidelines that crew members should know and comply at each stage of flight.

Chapter

5

At All Times

Regulations at all times are the rules that must be observed throughout the flight. Cabin crew is obliged to monitor the compliance of these regulations.

I. Crew Members Impairment/Incapacitation

If a crew member has a reasonable cause to suspect another crew member is impaired by alcohol or drugs or is physically incapable of job performance, it is imperative the issue should be resolved before departure. Crew members' incapacitation may occur any time, during any stage of flight. Early recognition is critical.

Suspect any incapacitation if a crew member does not respond to two verbal communications. Place the incapacitated crew member in an available seat. Provide first aid. Consider using deadheading crew members. All crew members are responsible for monitoring possible impairment and incapacitation of other crew members.

If Suspect Crew is:	Then Notify
Captain	First Officer
First Officer	Captain
Duty Purser	Captain
Cabin Crew	Duty Purser

American Airlines Pilot Dies Mid-Flight from Heart Attack

(Source: https://youtu.be/ouk9W2B-cDA)

II. Standard Communication Signals

Captains mainly communicate with cabin crew using on/off of the 'Fasten Seat Belt' sign during the flight.

Category	Standard Sign	Initiated by	Response
Take-off	Fasten Seat Belt Sign cycles 3 times	Captain	Cabin crew ensures: All passengers are seated. Cabin is ready for take-off. All cabin crew seated.
10,000ft Notification During Ascent	Fasten Seat Belt Sign	Captain	PA 'Seat belt fastened at all times recommendation'
Approaching	Fasten Seat Belt Sign cycles 3 times and the sign lights **off** or **on** PIC's PA 'Cabin crew, prepare for landing'	Captain	Cabin crew ensures: Prepare cabin for landing.
Landing During Descent	Fasten Seat Belt Sign cycles 3 times and the sign lights **on**	Captain	Cabin crew finally ensures: Cabin is ready for landing. All crews and passengers are seated. Sterile cockpit is initiated.
Brace Position Signals	Fasten Seat Belt Sign cycles 4 times	Captain	Cabin crew commands passengers to brace: "충격방지자세/Brace!"
Emergency Signals	3 consecutive bells on the interphone system	All Crews	Pick up the nearest handset.
If Evacuation is Required	Horn and flashing indicator light	Captain	Cabin crew ensures: Silence the alarm. Initiate evacuation immediately.

III. Weight & Balance

Weight and balance should be kept for the safe take-off/landing of aircrafts and efficient operations. Occasionally, due to weight and balance restrictions, some seat rows may not be occupied during the flight. The captain and ground staffs will advise cabin crew when these restrictions apply and which rows are affected. Although the rows will not be visibly blocked, cabin crews are to ensure seats in these blocked rows are not occupied at any time during the flight. If weight and balance is not observed, cases below may occur. In this case, passenger and cargo items are rearranged to the front.

Passenger Complaint

"Why does K Air always leave empty seats in the front, and assign the passengers in the back of the cabin?"

A: We apologize for this inconvenience, but please understand this situation. In order to make safe take-off and landing, the weight and balance should be made in the middle of the wing. However, the engine of this aircraft is attached in front of the wing. Those seats in the front should be empty. We will be pleased if you understand this situation.

IV. Smoking Regulations

Most airlines prohibit smoking on board. Passengers who don't comply with smoking regulations may get punished under the Aircraft Safety & Security Act. Airlines should undertake all possible safety precautions to bring to passengers' attention to the restrictions on smoking. Such precautions are:

- **Announcements over PA** systems prior to take-off
- Installation of **smoke detectors** in all lavatories to provide an alert of fire
- Installation of **'No Smoking'** placards on each side of lavatory doors
- Installation of **'No Cigarette Disposal'** placards on or near each waste disposal receptacle in all lavatories
- Installation of **ashtrays** on or near the entry side of all lavatory doors

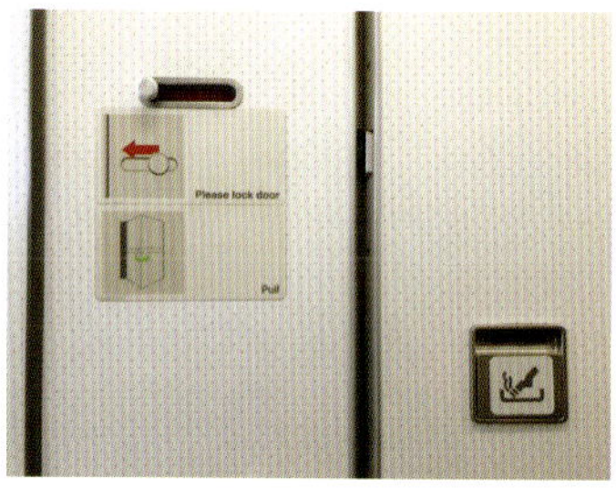

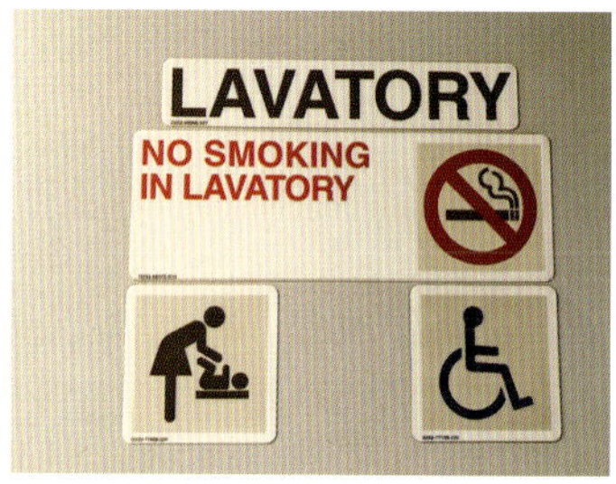

Man Jailed for Nine Years and Six Months for Smoking in Plane Toilet

(Source: https://metro.co.uk)

V. Use of Portable Electronic Devices (PED) and Restrictions

The Aviation Security Law restricts the use of certain devices in an aircraft to prevent interference with communication and/or navigation system. As the use of unauthorized electronic devices can cause interference with radio communication, navigation system, and airplane operational system, passengers shall be informed of PED restriction and comply with the regulation.

PIC (Pilot In Command) has the ultimate authority regarding PED use, and PIC may prohibit the use of approved PEDs in the case of any suspected or confirmed EMI (Electromagnetic Interference) event. Upon PIC's request, cabin crew shall not allow passengers to use the PEDs.

In case that a passenger does not comply with restriction of PED use, cabin crew shall advise the passenger his/her PED use affects flight safety and that noncompliance is illegal.

1. May Not Be Operated at Any Time

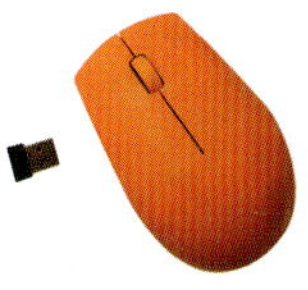

- AM/FM radio, television (portable TV receiver)
- Peripheral devices for computer connected by a cable (printer, fax)
  *exception: computer external mouse
- Remote control toys
- Wireless mouse (not Bluetooth mouse)
- Transmitters (citizen band or two-way, Walkie-talkie etc.)

2. May Be Operated When Aircraft Door is Open

- GPS receiver utilizing external wire
- Two-way pager
- PDA, smart devices (smart phone, tablet, e-reader etc.)
  with cellular transmitting function on, mobile phones

After aircraft push back and during extended ground delay, these devices may be authorized for use at the captain's discretion. However, the devices need to be set to airplane mode or the cellular service is turned off before the aircraft continues for flight.

3. May Be Operated at All Times

- Heart pacemaker, hearing aids, electronic nerve stimulator, implanted medical devices
- Personal life support systems, medical support devices
- Portable voice recorder, electric shaver, noise reduction headphone
- Airline installed equipment (telephone, video equipment etc.)
- GPS receivers that do not utilize external wires, one-way pagers

If visibility of the runway is below 550m, the PIC may advise the purser to restrict the use of the following PEDs:

- Smart devices (PDA, smart phone, tablet, e-reader etc.) in airplane mode or with cellular service off
- Electronic video player, Bluetooth devices, laptop computer
- Electronic camera, video recorders
- CO/MD/MP3 players, digital cassette players or recorders

VI. Handling Dangerous Goods

Dangerous goods are hazardous materials capable of posing a significant risk to human health, property, or the environment if not handled properly when transported by air. Dangerous goods shall not be placed in the cabin. When accepting and assisting with carry-on baggage, cabin crew should also monitor for dangerous goods. If a package is found in the cabin with a dangerous goods label or any of the suspicious signs listed below, cabin crew should question the passenger and notify the captain immediately.

- Not sealed properly
- Signs of leaking
- Peculiar odor

1. Classification and Hazard Labels

Dangerous goods are classified into the following 9 classes. They must have special labels affixed to each package. Labels are used to inform the type of dangerous goods and to identify the hazards at a glance. Each class has its own label.

1) Class 1: Explosive Substances

- Firearms and weapons carried by not-permitted persons, flares, ammunition etc.

2) Class 2: Gases

- liquefied, compressed, dissolved under pressure, deeply refrigerated
- Spray can, aerosol, butane cassettes, propane tanks, scuba tanks, oxygen tanks etc.

3) Class 3/4: Flammable Liquids/Solids

• Lots of matches or lighters, strike-anywhere matches, all fuels, paints, thinner, camping gears

4) Class 5: Oxidizing Substances and Organic Peroxides

5) Class 6: Toxic (Poisonous) and Infectious Substances

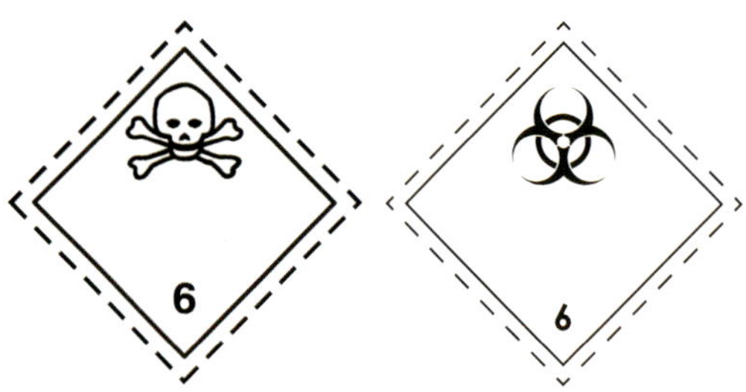

6) Class 7: Radioactive Materials

- Instruments containing radioactive source radioisotopes

7) Class 8: Corrosives

- Acids, alkalis, metallic mercury, wet-cell batteries, thermometers and barometers containing mercury

8) Class 9: Miscellaneous Dangerous Goods

- Magnetized materials, asbestos, formalin and other offensive/irritating substances liable to harm passenger or damage aircraft

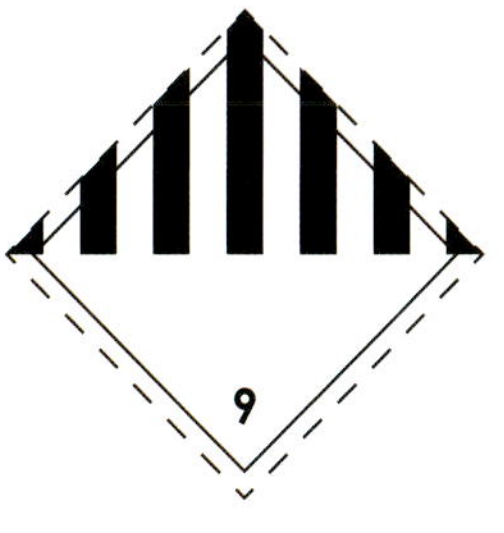

2. Handling Labels

• Magnetized Material

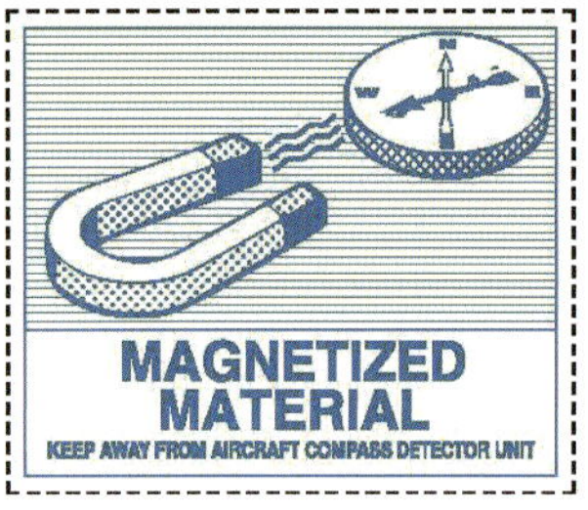

• Cargo Aircraft Only

• Cryogenic Liquid

• Environmentally Hazardous Substance

• Radioactive Material- Excepted Package

• Keep Away From Heat

• Package Orientation

• Lithium Battery Label

• Limited Quantities Mark

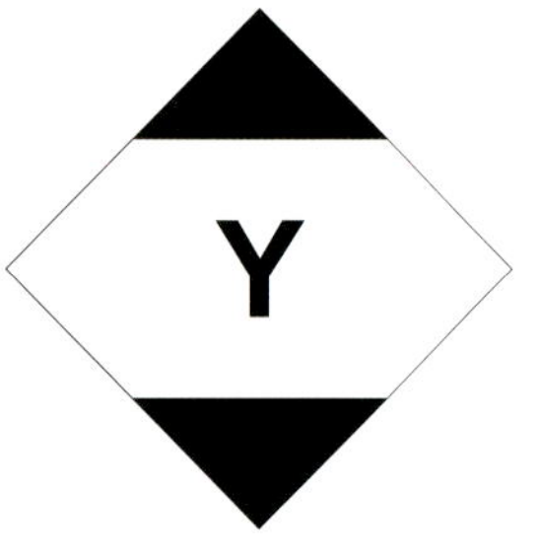

3. Dangerous Goods Accepted in the Aircraft

In the interest of safety, prohibited goods must not be carried in any baggage (checked or carry-on). Some dangerous goods can be carried as cargo and carry-on baggage provided the applicable conditions mandated on IATA Dangerous Goods Regulations (DGR) and ICAO Technical Instruction (TI), for their carriage has been met.

1) Acceptable as Carry-on Baggage

- Alcohol not exceeding 5 liters (24% - 70%)
- Aerosols (perfume, hair spray, medicine containing alcohol)
- 1 medical thermometer (protective case)
- 1 safety match or 1 cigarette lighter
- Dry ice (2.5kg, for packing perishables)
- Mercury barometer or thermometer (carried by representative of a government)
- Medical oxygen cylinder (5kg, liquid oxygen are forbidden)

2) Acceptable as Checked Baggage

- Ammunition (securely packaged by DGR)
- Camping stove (empty fuel tank/container)
- Battery powered wheelchair
  - Battery must be separated
  - Record in NOTOC (Notification To Captain) and notify to captain

  *Lithium ion battery (for powered wheelchair) must be removed and carried in the cabin.

3) Exceptions

The following do not apply to dangerous goods.

- Placed on board with the approval of the operator to provide medical aid to a patient during flight (AED: containing lithium batteries)
- Dangerous goods that are required in accordance with the operating regulations (e.g. fire extinguishers)

Student Activity - **Team Discussion**

Read the article and answer the questions.

Crash: Asiana B744 near Jeju on July 28th 2011, fire in cargo hold

(Source: http://avherald.com)

Q1. What caused the accident?

Q2. What kinds of dangerous goods should be labeled as follows?

Q3. During boarding, if you find the passenger who has the box below, what action should you take? Can this passenger fly with his baggage?

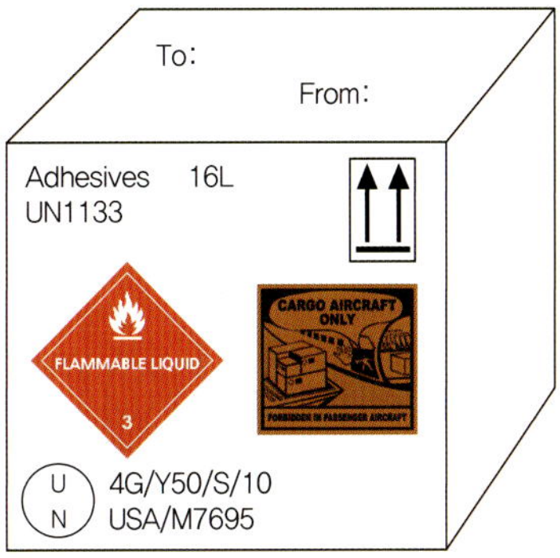

Chapter

6

Pre-Flight

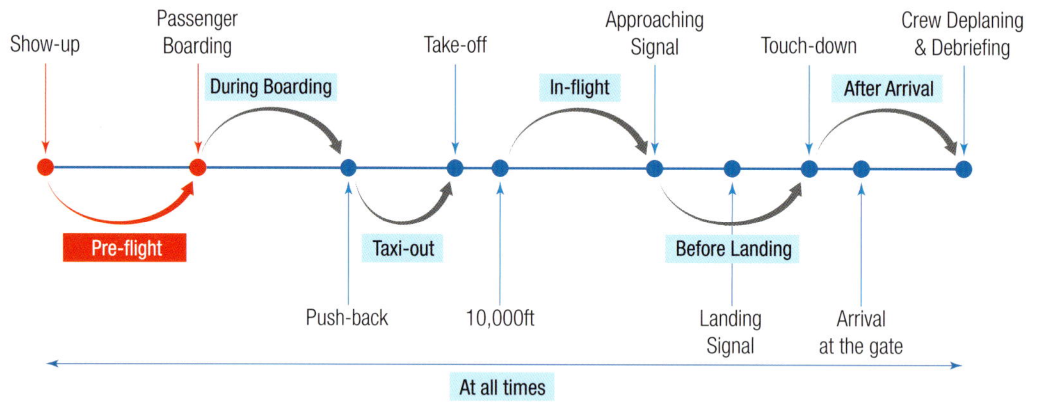

Pre-flight refers to the period from cabin briefing to before passenger boarding. During pre-flight, cabin crew must attend the cabin briefing and joint briefing and conduct the pre-flight check.

I. Cabin Briefing

Cabin crews are required to participate in the cabin briefing conducted by the duty purser at the designated place and time. Cabin crews must prepare for the flight before participating in the cabin briefing.

1. Topics to Be Covered

- Confirming (minimum) staffing for aircraft and check crew list (introductions)
- Check the necessary items for flight:
  Valid passport, visa, crew registration card, ID card and other entry documents for destination country
- Flight information:
  Special passenger information, flight time, time difference, aircraft type and registration number, destination information, related regulations/laws, C.I.Q. etc.
- Recent directives:
  Safety/Security issue which can affect crew and passengers, any changed/updated standards/procedures, equipment and system information, etc.

II. Joint Briefing

After the cabin briefing, cabin crews are required to participate in a joint briefing with the cockpit crew at a designated place and time. During the joint briefing, captain covers these topics:

- Security consideration
- Planned flight time, altitude and route
- En-route and destination weather, expected turbulence
- Passenger reservation status
- Cockpit entry procedures
- Sterile cockpit procedures
- Safety consideration ('Fasten Seat Belt' sign procedure, PA procedure for turbulence)
- Emergency procedures

Joint Briefing Scenario

Good morning everyone, my name is Jang HyungSu and I'm the pilot in command in this flight. Flight No is KE081 bound for New York.
Departure time is 10:00(+9) and Arrival time is 10:05(-4). Time difference between Seoul and New York is 13 hours. New York is 13 hours behind Seoul. Flight time is 12 hours 37 minutes. The departure weather is rainy, windy, with the temperature 12℃. Turbulence is expected after 15 minutes of take-off and cabin crew should remain seated in your jumpseat until I turn off the seat belt sign. I will make an announcement after take-off to passengers about the anticipated turbulence and ask the cabin crew to remain seated until advised. The arrival weather is expected to be cloudy, with the temperature 15℃. Aircraft is A380 and the capacity is 12/94/300, passenger reservation status is 12/67/298. After pre-flight check, please let me know if something is wrong. Security level is alert 3 and please observe sterile cockpit regulations. Cockpit entry procedure is interphone first, then knock 3 times. Have a nice flight!

III. Security Check and Crew Boarding

After joint briefing, crew members move to the airport and board the aircraft via CIQ area. At least 55 minutes before departure, crew members should board the aircraft.

Only the following are permitted to enter aircraft.

- Duty or extra flight crew and cabin crew who have a valid ID
- Airline employees or ground service personnel who have a valid ID and carry out official duties for the flight
- Passengers with proper boarding pass of the flight

IV. Stowage of Cabin Crew Baggage

Cabin crew should comply with carry-on baggage regulations with their own baggage. Cabin crew carry-on baggage should be stowed under the last seats of each zone. If not enough space is available, stow in overhead bin or coatroom.

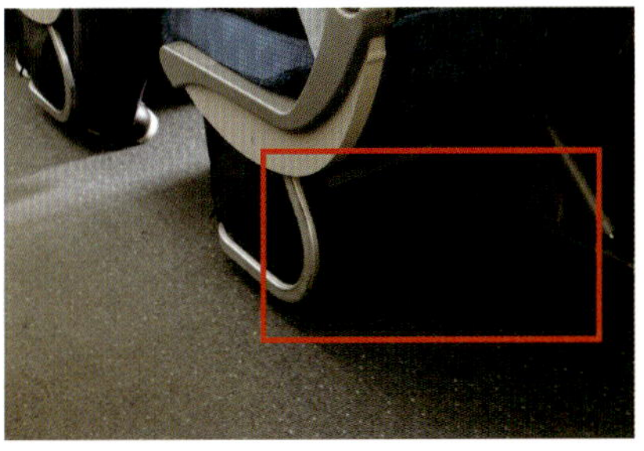

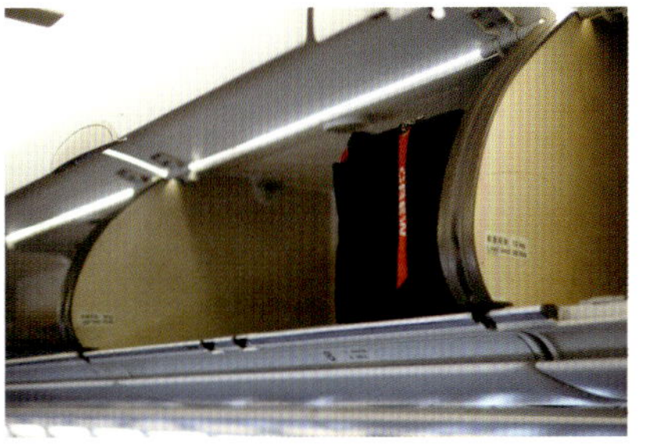

V. Pre-Flight Check

1. Equipment and System Check

Prior to each flight, the cabin crew should ensure that all safety equipment in the cabin is operative. They should check that the safety/security equipment is available, accessible, ready for use and secured in its designated stowage location. Cabin crew also check the system and other equipment in the cabin during the pre-flight check to ensure they are in good condition. The galley should be checked as part of the equipment check. Galley checks should also include verification of electrical equipment in the galley and security checks or searches of stowage areas.

The minimum required number of cabin crew for each aircraft should perform the pre-flight check in their assigned zone, and report to duty purser immediately when any discrepancy is found. In the event of any discrepancy, the Minimum Equipment List (MEL) that details the systems and equipment required for operation is used by the crew and maintenance personnel to verify details as to which equipment should be operational, under what conditions, for a flight to be dispatched. It also lists the items that may be missing or inoperative, as applicable to each aircraft type.

• **B737-800 (73HT)**

Emergency Equipment	Quantity
First Aid Kit	3
Halon Type Extinguisher	2+1
H_2O type Extinguisher	1
Megaphone	2
PO_2 Bottle	5
PBE	4+1

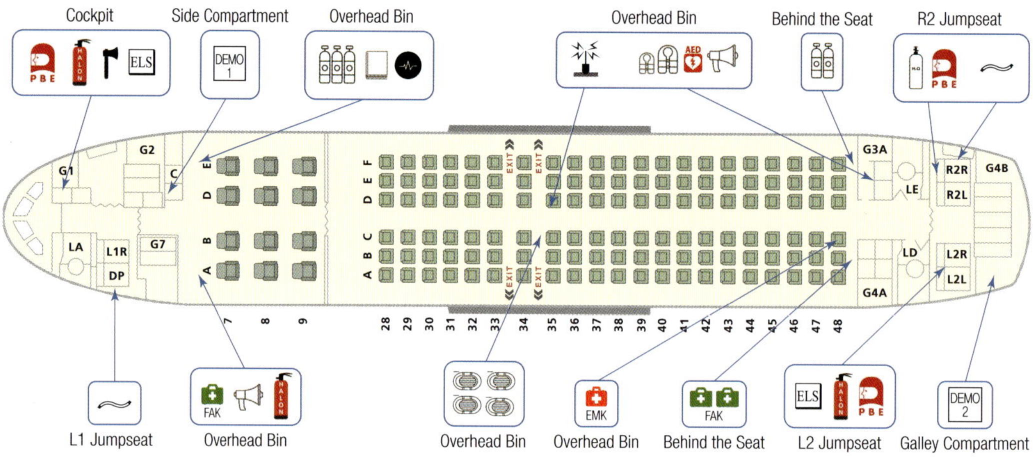

The checklist below shows what should be checked during the pre-flight check. Cabin crew should be aware of emergency equipment in their assigned zones. Emergency equipment is categorized into 5 parts which are first aid equipment, smoke and fire equipment, safety equipment, security equipment, evacuation and ditching equipment. Let's look into each equipment in detail.

Pre-flight Equipment Checklist

Equipment		What to Check	
Crew Life Vest		· In place · Quantity and condition	
Flashlight	Auto Type	· In place · Blinking red light or green light on LED	
PO_2 (Portable Oxygen Bottle)		· In place · Tube fitting plugged into outlet · Gauge registers minimum 1600PSI	
PBE (Protective Breathing Equipment)		Puritan	· In place · ID tag (vacuum packing)
		Scott	· In place

H_2O Extinguisher	· In place · Wire seal intact
Halon Extinguisher	· In place · Wire or plastic seat intact · Pressure gauge (green band)
Megaphone	· In place · Sound · Properly secured
ELT (Emergency Locator Transmitter)	· In place
FAK (First Aid Kit)	· In place · Lead seal or tape seal intact
Seat Belt Extension	· In place
Infant/Spare Life Vest	· In place · Quantity and condition (if the number of passengers exceeds the number of seats)
Cabin Log (CL)	· In place
ELS (Emergency Light Switch)	· Location
EMK (Emergency Medical Kit)	· In place · Seal intact
Resuscitator Bag, UPK (Universal Precaution Kit)	· In place
Automatic Sphygmomanometer	· In place
Fireproof Glove	· In place
AED (Automated External Defibrillator)	· In place · Battery (hourglass)
Smoke Detector (external)	· Location · Ensure detecting part is clear
Passenger Briefing Equipment	· In place · Quantity and condition
Life Raft (if applicable)	· In place · Quantity and condition

Security Equipment

Equipment	What to Check
Tie Wrap/Rope/Explosion-Proof Mat/Explosion-Proof Jacket	· In place · Seal intact
Hijack Warning Bell	· Location

1) First Aid Equipment

A variety of emergency medical equipment and supplies should be kept on board in accordance with operator policies and authority regulations.

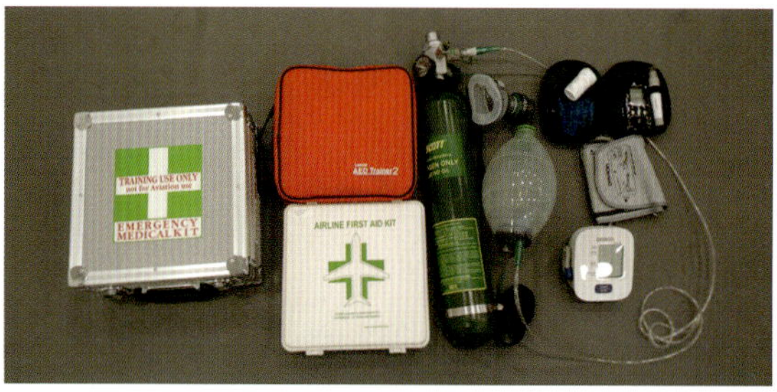

(1) PO_2 (Portable Oxygen Bottle)

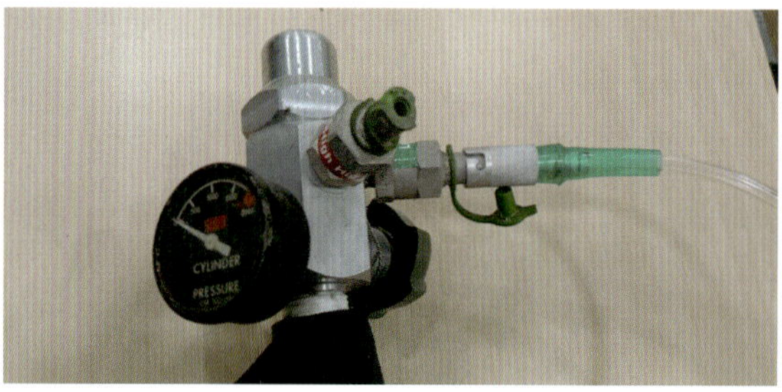

Portable oxygen bottles are on board in accordance with regulatory requirements. They are used to supply oxygen for supplemental (decompression) and first aid. During the pre-flight check, cabin crew should check whether oxygen bottle is in place, the tube fitting is well connected to the PO_2 outlet, and the pressure gauge is higher than 1600 psi. For use, ensure tube fitting is securely plugged into the outlet, turn the knob to the left (counter-clockwise), place the mask over nose and mouth, secure the mask with the elastic band, and monitor oxygen use. Never allow any PO_2 bottle to empty.

(2) EMK (Emergency Medical Kit)

EMK is used to provide advanced medical equipment and medications in case of in-flight medical emergency. Check point is in place and red seal intact. The equipment and medications in the EMK can be used by medical personnel (doctor, nurse, dentist, oriental medical doctor, and maternity nurse) only who have medical knowledge or skills necessary to use items in the kit. Before use cabin crew should report to the captain.

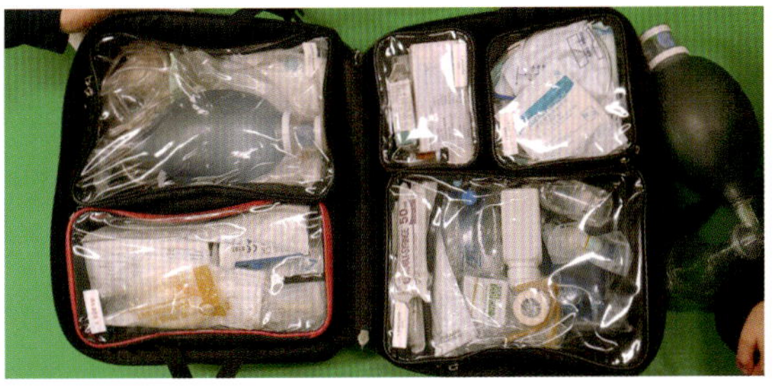

(3) Resuscitator Bag

Resuscitator bag contains bag valve mask for providing oxygen, thermometer and sphygmomanometer for checking the vital signs. Resuscitator bag is tied to the handle of EMK. Inside the resuscitator bag, there are bag valve mask (mask with one-way valve), elastic bandage, electronic thermometer, UPK (Universal Precaution Kit), stethoscope sphygmomanometer (manual), needle disposable box, passenger health condition checklist, and ice pack.

(4) UPK (Universal Precaution Kit)

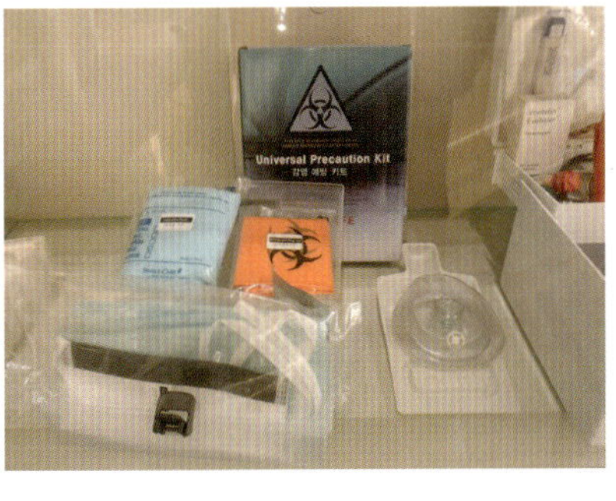

UPK is used to reduce the possibility of contamination by contact with body fluids (including blood) and to clean up the area contaminated by body fluids. UPK is placed in the resuscitator bag. The contents of a universal precaution kit would typically include:

- Dry powder that can convert a small liquid spill into a granulated gel
- Germicidal disinfectant for surface cleaning

- Skin wipes, face/eye mask (separate or combined)
- Gloves (disposable), bio-hazard disposal waste bag
- Impermeable full-length long-sleeved gown that fastens at the back
- Large absorbent towel, pick-up scoop with scraper, instructions

(5) AED (Automated External Defibrillator)

AED is used to provide an effective method of restoring normal heart rhythm following sudden cardiac arrest or tachycardia from ventricular fibrillation. All aircraft are equipped with AED. Check if it is in place and its battery (hourglass). AED can be used by physicians and emergency medical workers. If there is no physician or emergency medical worker on board, cabin crew trained for AED can use it. AED can be used for all ages, but when you use for an infant (less than 12 months of age), place the pad in the center of chest and center of back.

For use, first turn the power on, and apply pads to patient's chest. And then connect pads connector to AED. The moment of applying the pad to the patient's chest, AED starts analyzing patient's heart rhythm. During analyzing, do not touch the patient. If shock is needed, charging is started. During charging, you should keep doing CPR. After charging is finished, shock should be delivered. Before pressing the shock button, you must say "stay away from the patient". AED analyzes patient heart rhythm every two minutes. Once you start CPR, you must not stop CPR until the patient's heartbeat returns.

(6) FAK (First Aid Kit)

FAK is used to provide basic first aid supplies for medical accidents of passengers by crew members or medical personnel. The check point is in place and seal intact (wire of tape). FAK is required to be loaded in the passenger aircraft by Aviation Act. FAK can be used without doctor's prescription, but before use, it must be reported to the captain.

•AED

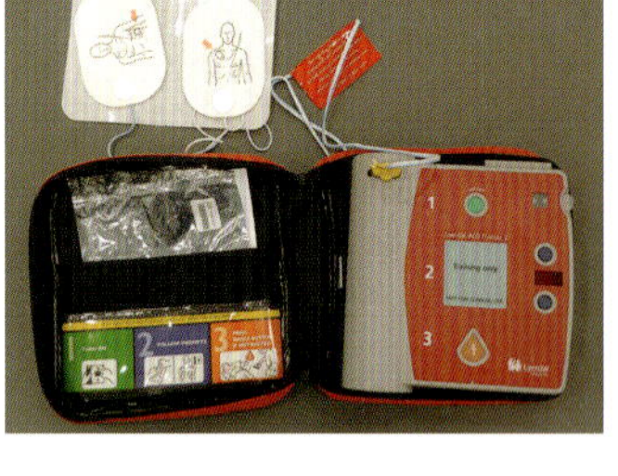

•FAK

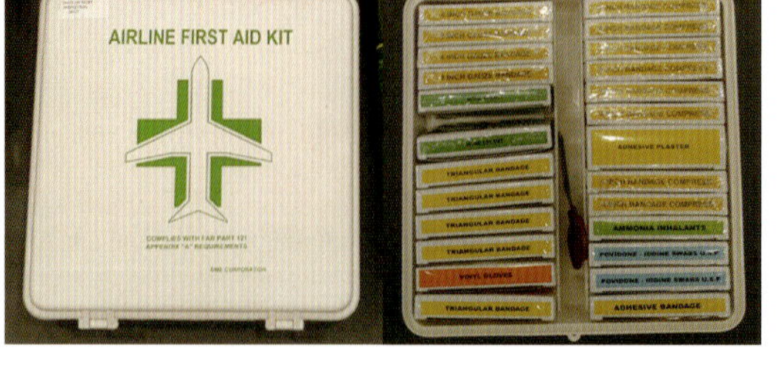

First Aid Flow Chart

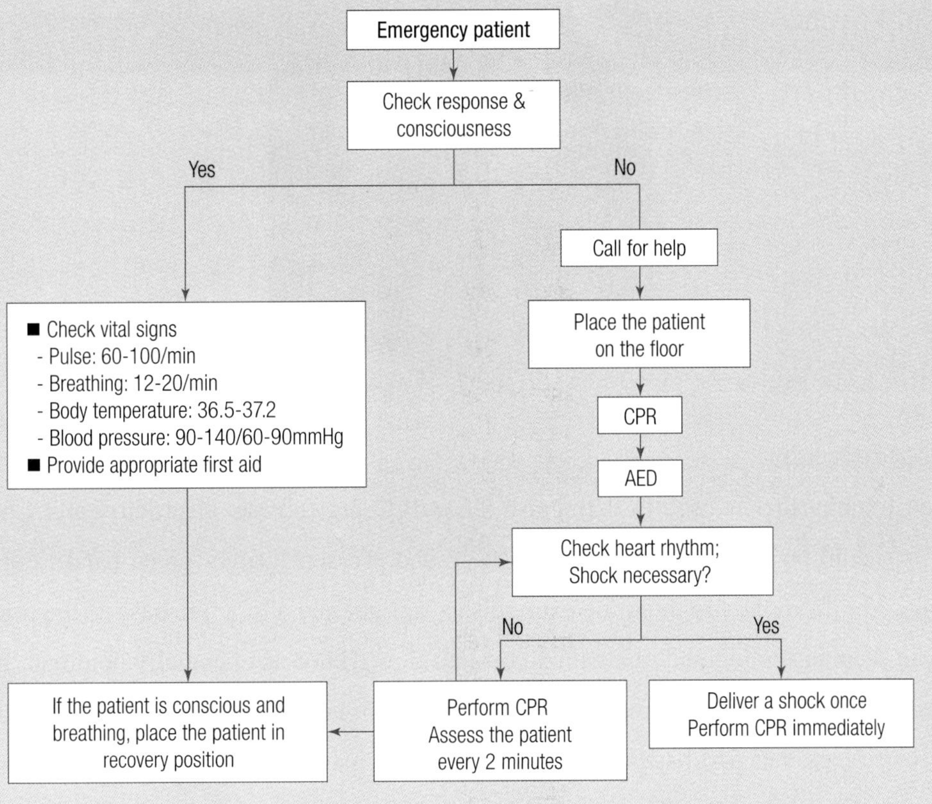

2) Smoke and Fire Equipment

There is a high possibility of fire as much as emergency patients during the flight. Failure to extinguish in-flight fires can lead to catastrophes. So it is important to know what kinds of smoke and fire equipment are on board and how to use it. There are 3 elements of fire which are fuel, heat and oxygen. To extinguish the fire, you just remove one of these (refer to Chapter 10).

(1) H_2O Extinguisher

H_2O Extinguisher is used to extinguish Class A fire (solid materials such as papers, clothes, baggage etc.). It should be in place and its wire seal intact. For use, fully turn the handle to the right, press the thumb lever while holding the extinguisher upright and aim at the base of the fire. Do not use for fire caused by grease or electricity because it may spread the fire or cause electric shock. An anti-freeze compound is added to the water, making it hazardous for drinking. Discharge lasts for approximately 40 seconds.

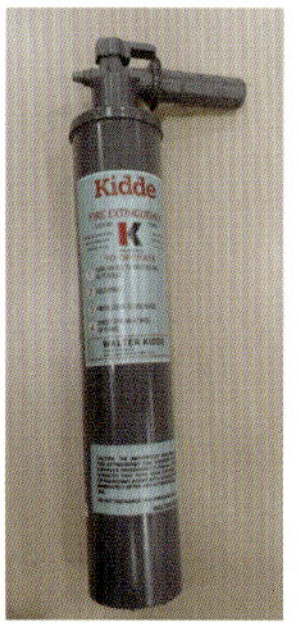

(2) Halon Extinguisher

Halon Extinguisher is used to extinguish Class B/C fire (grease, electricity) and Class A fire. It should be in place, with its seal intact, and pressure gauge (green band). For use, stand 2 - 3m from the fire, hold the extinguisher upright and aim at the base of the fire, use a rapid seeping motion and maintain a constant flow. Halon is essentially nontoxic. It can be sprayed on a person on fire, if necessary. However, do not use on a face. If used on Class A fire (papers, clothes and baggage etc.), ensure halon blast will not further spread burning materials. Discharge lasts for approximately 10 - 20 seconds.

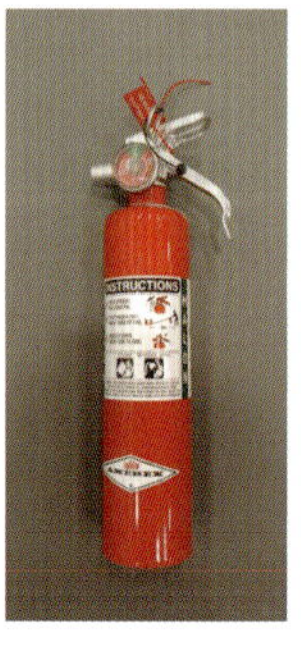
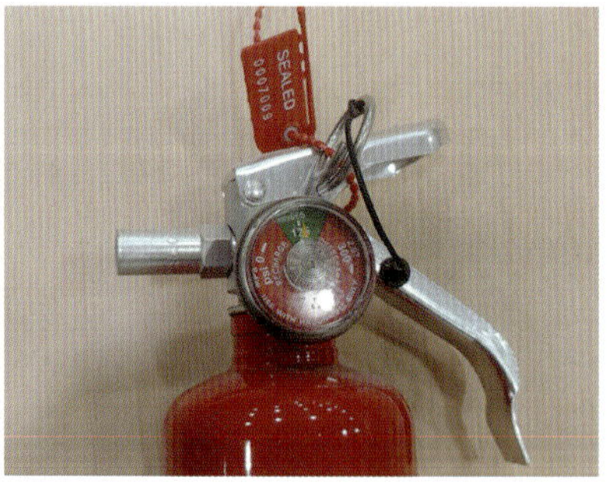

(3) Heat Activated Halon Extinguisher

Heat activated halon extinguisher is mounted in the lavatory trash receptacle to extinguish lavatory trash receptacle fires. These are designed to activate automatically when heat is present in the waste bin. Heat activated halon extinguisher automatically emits halon when temperature reaches approximately 80°C.

(4) PBE (Protective Breathing Equipment)

PBE is used to protect cabin crew from smoke inhalation and toxic fumes when fighting an in-flight fire and improve visibility in a smoke-filled cabin. The check point is in place and ID tag. There are three types of PBE which are Puritan PBE, Scott PBE and Essex PBE. The provided oxygen lasts for approximately 15 minutes. Never remove hood before leaving fire area.

• **Scott PBE**

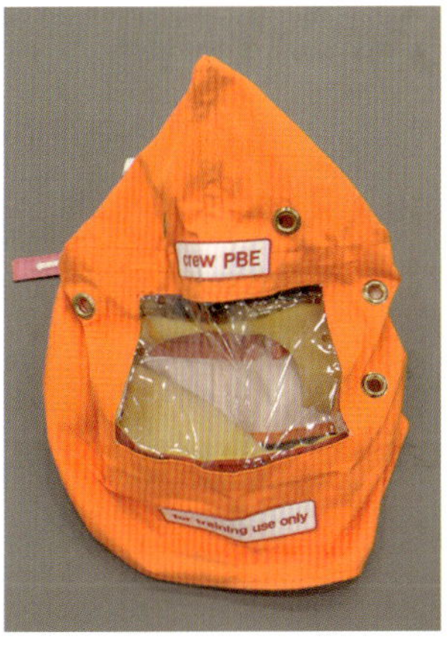

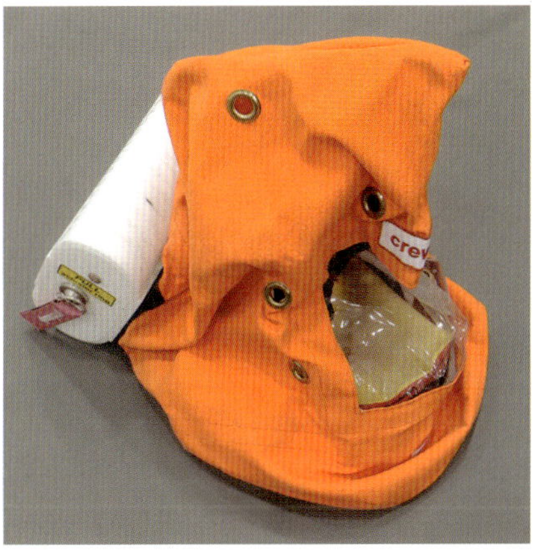

• **Puritan PBE**

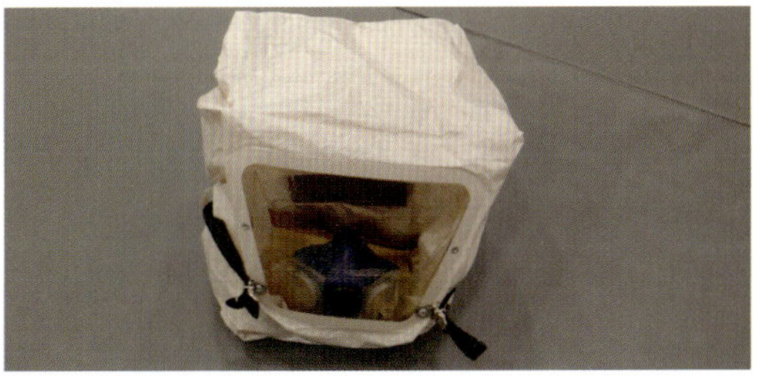
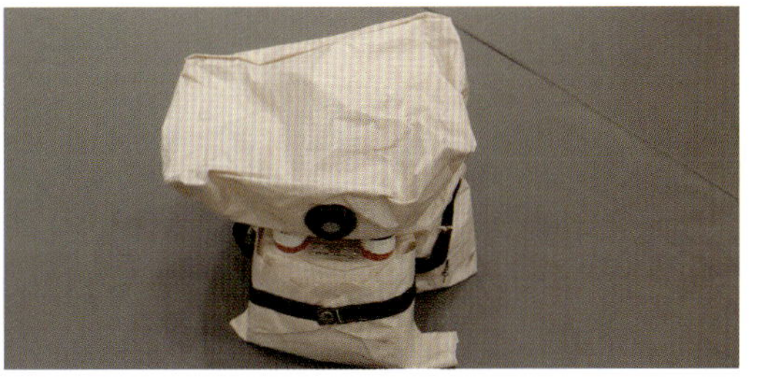

• Essex PBE

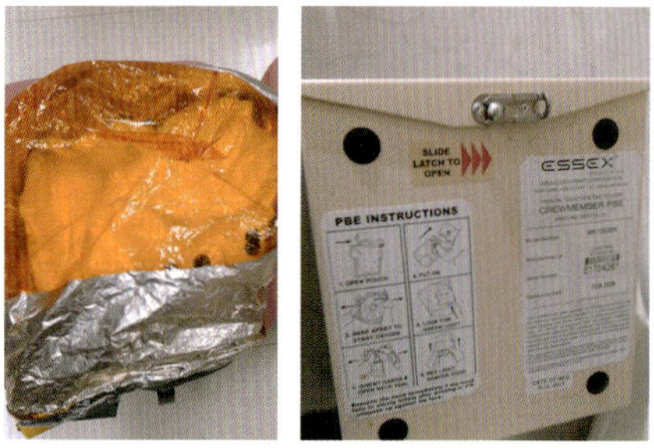

• PBE in Cabin

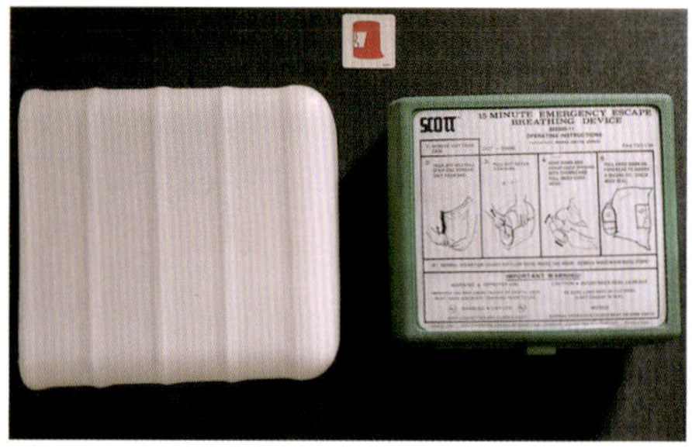

(5) Smoke Detector

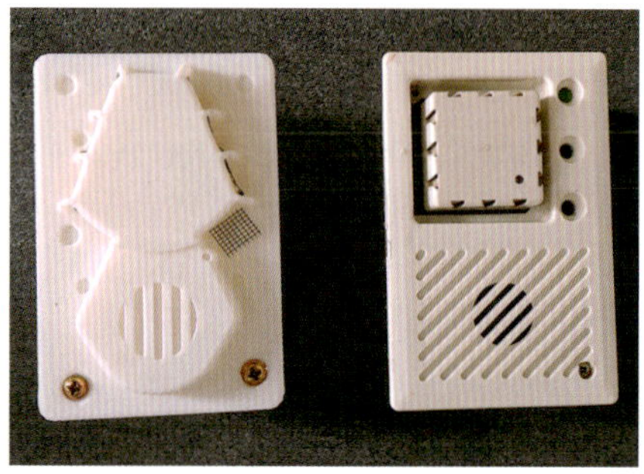

Aircraft are fitted with smoke detectors in the lavatories and crew rest areas. It is used to indicate the presence of smoke in the lavatory and crew rest areas and provide a warning light on the flight deck and in the cabin (audio and/or light). The check point is its location and needs to ensure detecting part is clear. When the smoke detector in the lavatories activates, immediately check for any smoke or fire in the lavatory. If a passenger has smoked in the lavatory, cabin crew should visually check that the cigarette has been put out completely and report it to captain. If the lavatory is occupied by the passenger who smoked, ask him or her to refrain from smoking, notifying that smoking in lavatory is prohibited by law. If the lavatory is not occupied, follow the fire-fighting procedures (refer to the chapter 10).

(6) Fireproof Gloves

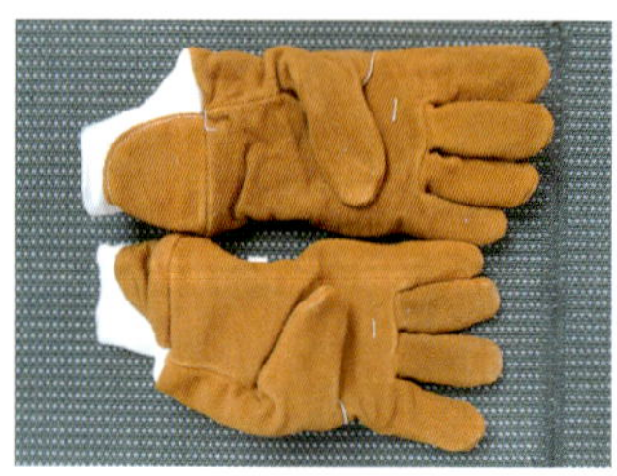

Fireproof gloves are used to prevent burns to hands or arms during the fire-fighting.

(7) Crash Axe

Crash axe is stored on the aircraft as for regulatory requirements and security considerations. Passengers should not be able to identify the location of the axe through placarding, so crash axe is stored in the cockpit. If a fire occurs inside the panel or cabin structure that is inaccessible, use it to remove those obstructions. Before using the crash axe, cabin crew should communicate with captain to prevent unwanted damage.

(8) Emergency Power-Off Switch

Emergency power-off switch is used to shut off total galley power in the event of an abnormal galley fire situation.

(9) Circuit Breaker

Circuit breaker is a black button and used to prevent a fire caused by electric overload. If the equipment is overloaded, the circuit breaker automatically pops out and cuts off the equipment power. Pull out the circuit breaker in the event of a fire or if necessary. If a circuit breaker pops out, notify to the captain. It can be reset by captain's instruction. To reset, push the circuit breaker. The circuit breaker that has been reset should be marked to be recognized. The circuit breaker can be reset only one time.

3) Safety Equipment

(1) Jumpseat with Seat Belt & Shoulder Harness

Jumpseat with seat belt and shoulder harness is to avoid or minimize injuries in an impact by securing crew members seated in the jumpseat. Only authorized cabin crew may occupy a jumpseat. A jumpseat which does not fold automatically is considered inoperative. The inoperative jumpseat must not be occupied and should be placed in the retracted position.

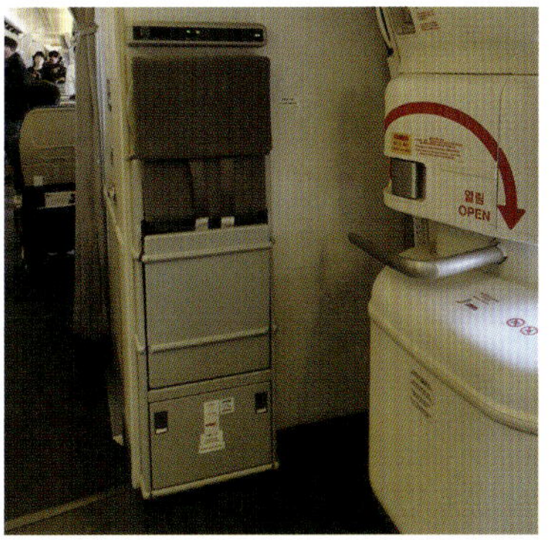

(2) Seat Belt Extension

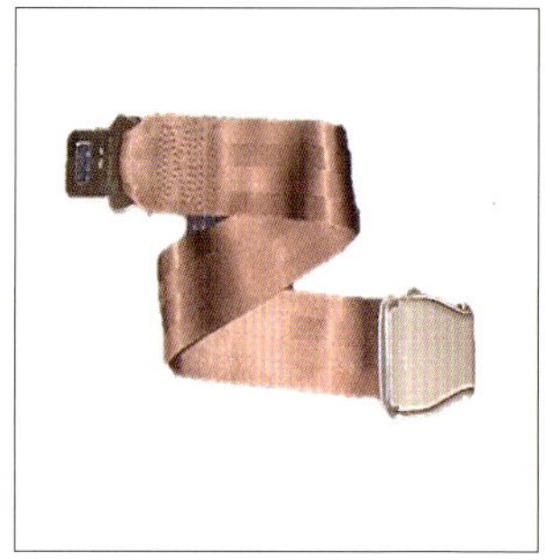

All aircraft passenger seats are equipped with a seat belt. However, seat belt extension is used by passengers when the length of a normal seat belt is insufficient. It is not for cabin crew to use on the jumpseat, but it can be used to secure cabin reserved seat baggage or child restraint device.

(3) Safety Information Card

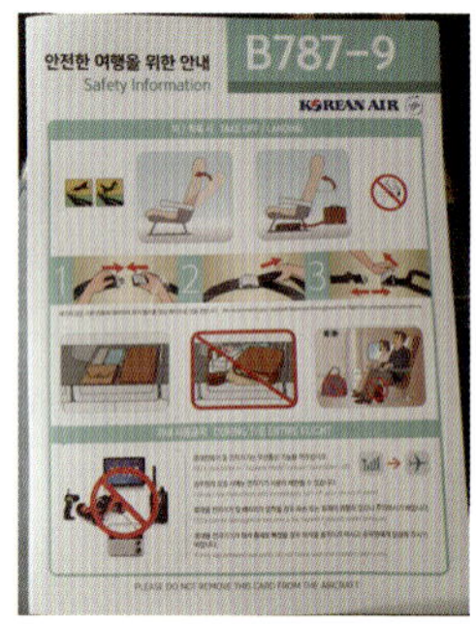

A passenger safety information card must be located at each seat and must be visible from the seated position. Operators may provide braille and/or large print safety cards for passengers who are visually impaired. These may be distributed to visually impaired passengers during their personal pre-flight safety briefing. Airlines shall have a process to ensure that the correct and most up-to-date version of the safety card is installed on each aircraft.

Safety information card is to provide necessary safety information. It includes the contents of seat belt, emergency exits, life vest, passenger oxygen mask, emergency escape path lighting, smoking restriction, countermeasures against smoke in cabin and etc. Spare safety information cards are loaded on aircraft. If a passenger seat without a safety information card is found, provide it immediately.

4) Security Equipment

(1) Restraint Devices

Some airlines provide restraining handcuffs, tie-wraps, rope for cabin crew to use in the event that an unruly passenger requires restraining. Cabin crew should be trained on how to use these restraining devices.

(2) Air Taser/Gas Gun

Air Taser is loaded all the time on some airlines to control an unruly passenger who threatens the safety of passengers and crew members.

(3) Explosion-Proof Equipment

Explosion-proof mat and explosion-proof jacket are loaded to handle any bombs. It minimizes the damage by explosives, if found on board. In case of handling explosives in flight, a cabin crew designated by duty purser wears the explosion-proof jacket and handles the explosives.

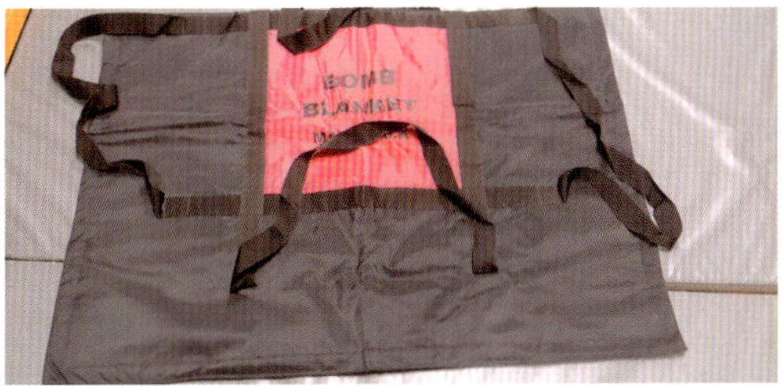

5) Evacuation and Ditching Equipment

(1) Emergency Lighting Switch (ELS)

The aircraft is fitted with an emergency lighting system to assist passengers and crew during an evacuation in both dark and smoke-filled cabins. ELS is used to activate the emergency lighting (escape path, cabin and exterior emergency lighting) that provide visual help in an emergency evacuation. Emergency lights are activated by pushing the ELS in the cockpit or in the Cabin Attendant Panel. Emergency lights are also automatically activated with a loss of electrical power.

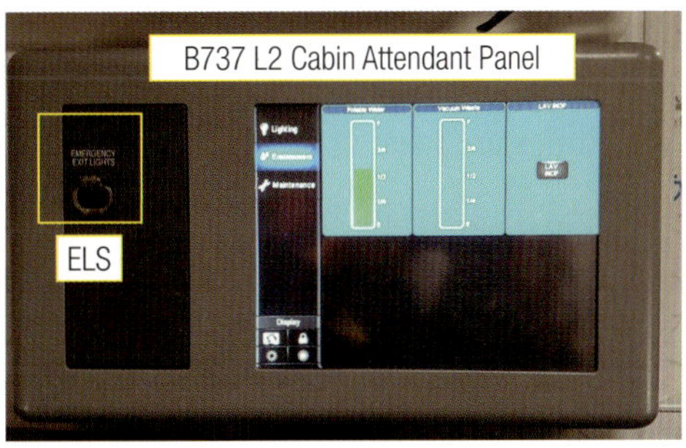

(2) Life Vest

All passenger seats and crew seats are equipped with a life vest. There are two kinds of

life vest, one is for an adult and the other is for an infant. These are usually found under each passenger seat or in the armrest (premium cabin), at cabin crew seats and in designated stowage locations (i.e., for infant life vests and additional adult/child life vests). Life vests are reversible. In order to deflate the life vest, press down on the valve built into the oral inflation tubes and squeeze the life vest to force air out. Life vests are equipped with a locator light. To activate a locator light, pull the center tab labeled 'Pull to Light'. The light will illuminate within a few seconds and will continue for 8 - 10 hours.

(3) Flashlight

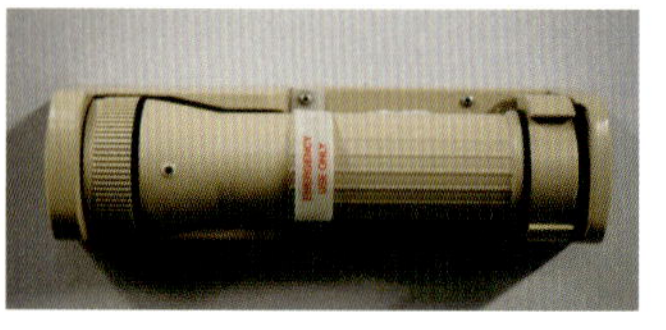

Flashlight is to direct, signal, and provide visual help in emergency situations only. The life of the flashlight is no less than 30 minutes and up to a maximum of 2 hours.

(4) Megaphone

Cabin crew can communicate and signal to passengers in an emergency with a megaphone (battery-operated).

(5) Escape Device (Slide and Slide/Raft)

Escape device is used to evacuate passengers and crew members from aircraft in emergencies. Slides or slide/rafts are installed on the inside of the cabin door, or externally inside the fuselage of the aircraft. Slides are used in an emergency land evacuation, and it is also used as a flotation device in ditching. Slide/rafts are used in the emergency land and ditching evacuation. They are designed to inflate automatically within a few seconds when opening a door in armed mode.

Slides and slide/rafts are usually fitted with a manual inflation mechanism that allows cabin crew to inflate the slide if the automatic system fails. Slides and slide/rafts are often fitted with:

- Manual inflation handle to ensure escape device inflation
- Ditching release handle(s) to allow release from the aircraft
- Mooring line with breakpoint
- Knife

First Class Photography / Shutterstock.com

©Getty Images Bank

Manual Inflation Handle

All inflatable escape devices such as slide, slide/raft, and life raft have a red manual inflation handle. This is to ensure escape device inflation.

Ditching Release Handle

It is located under a flap covering girt bar and is to detach the escape device from the girt bar end of the door sill of the aircraft. Unsnap and raise the flap, and pull ditching release handle. The weight of the escape device will cause the girt lacing to unravel; the device will drop away from the door.

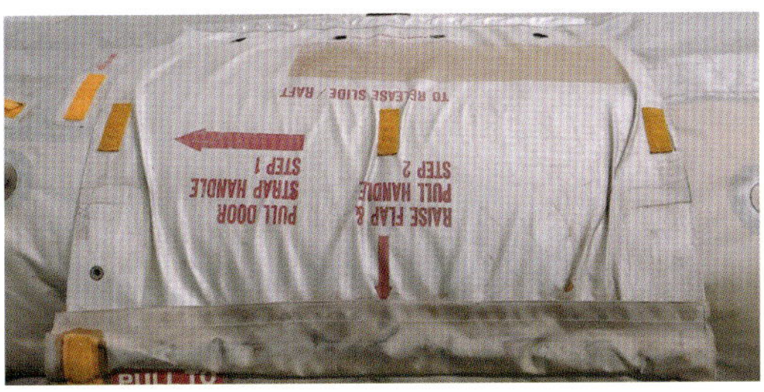

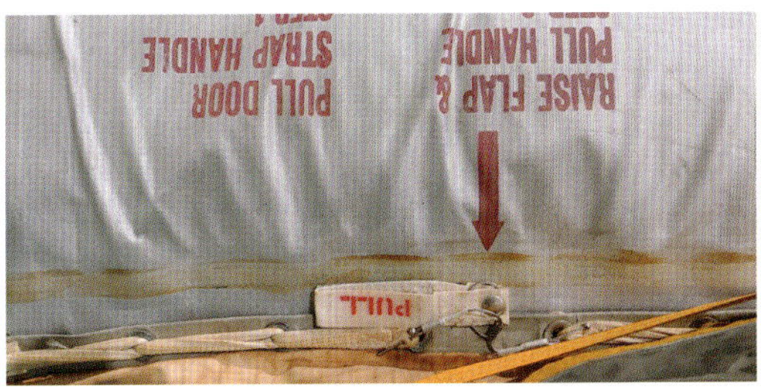

Mooring Line

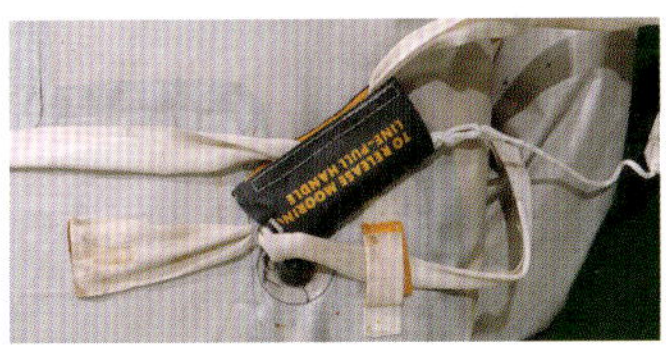

It is a line to re-enter aircraft after evacuation. It connects the detached escape device with aircraft. Cut mooring line to remove the escape device from the aircraft completely.

Knife

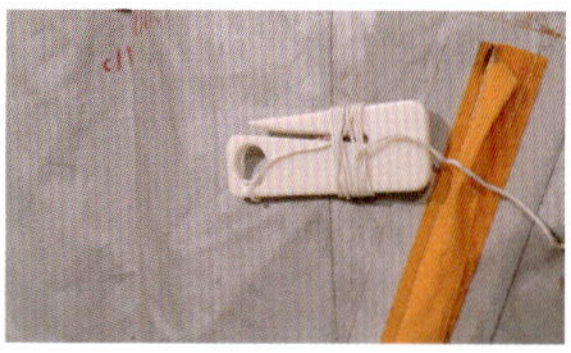

Located near the mooring line and use to cut the mooring line, detaching raft from the aircraft.

(6) Life Raft (Remote Raft)

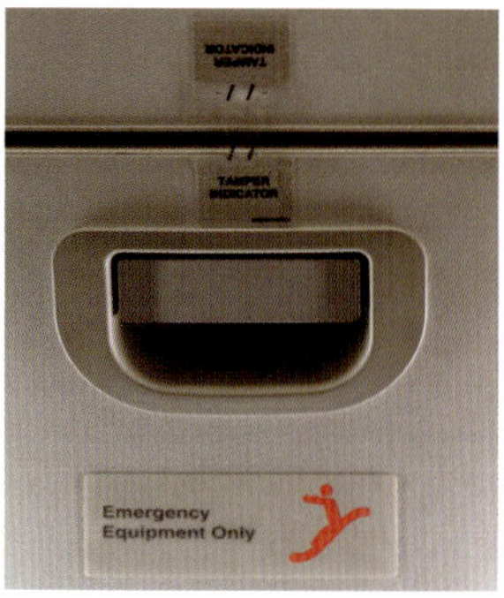

Where slide/raft capacity is not sufficient to accommodate all persons on board, or in the event of long range overwater operations of aircrafts which are not equipped with slide/raft, additional life rafts may be required. These are typically installed in overhead/ceiling compartments in the cabin.

(7) Escape Device Accessory

Emergency survival equipment is typically installed in a pack inside the slide/raft or life raft containing equipment such as:

Heaving Line

It is used to pull people out of the water and to tie slide/rafts together. A heaving line with a rubber ring is attached to the slide/raft.

Sea Anchor

Sea anchor is used to keep the raft near the ditching site, reducing the risk of capsizing.

ELT (Emergency Locator Transmitter)

Emergency locator transmitters may be fixed to the aircraft and automatically activated. Portable transmitters may also be carried and activated manually by cabin crew following an emergency landing away from an airport. It provides a signal to identify location for rescue.

Locator Light

Locator light activates when the slides or slide/rafts are inflated. It is positioned near the boarding stations to provide assistance to passengers trying to board the raft from the water.

Survival Kit

Survival (signaling and life-saving equipment) kit is equipped for using in land/water emergency and areas which the Authority designates as search and rescue would be especially difficult. On all slide/raft and raft, the survival kit is tied to the raft, floating separately. Contents are as follows.

- **Packaged Drinking Water**

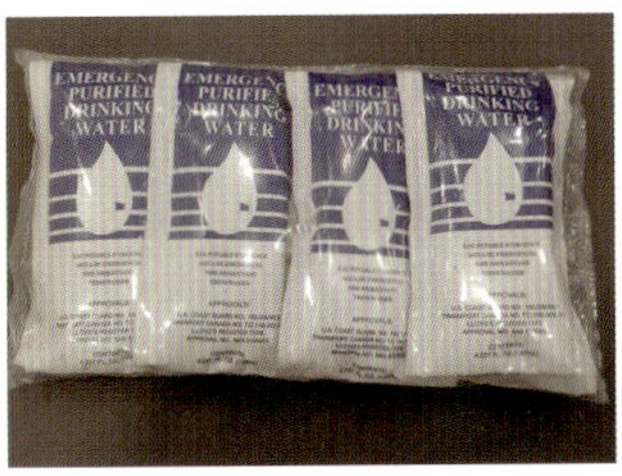

- **Purification Tablet**

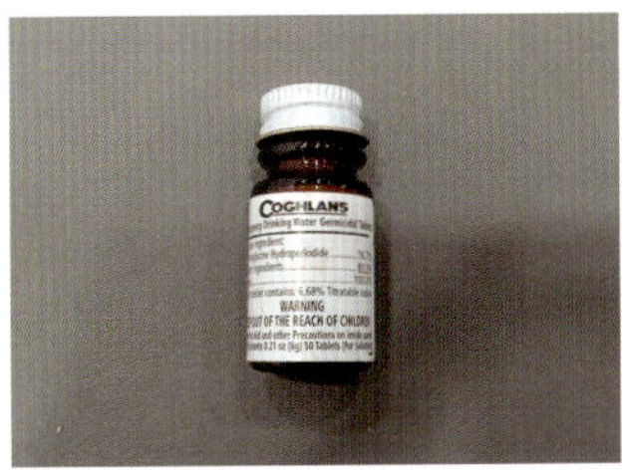

- **Repair Clamp**

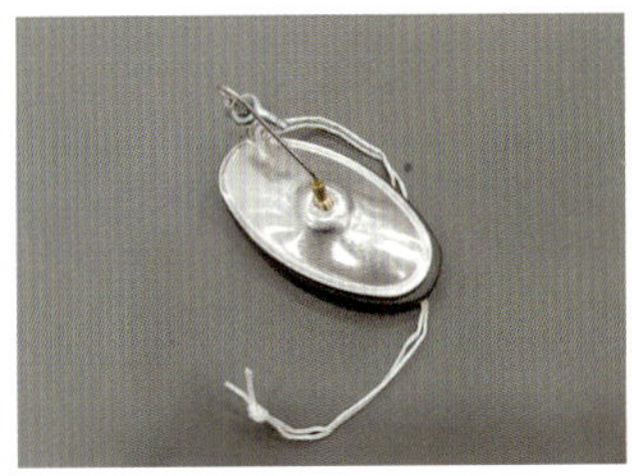

- **Smoke/Flare Kit**

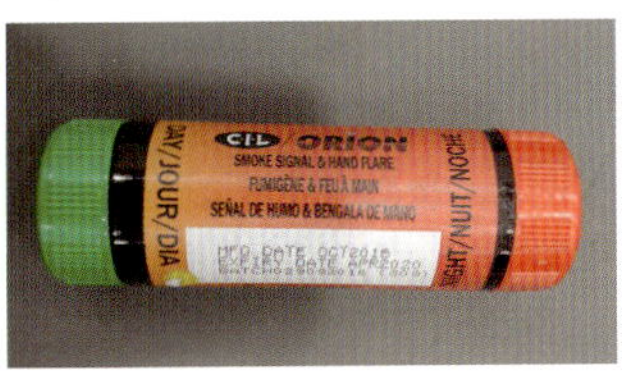

- **Utility Knife**

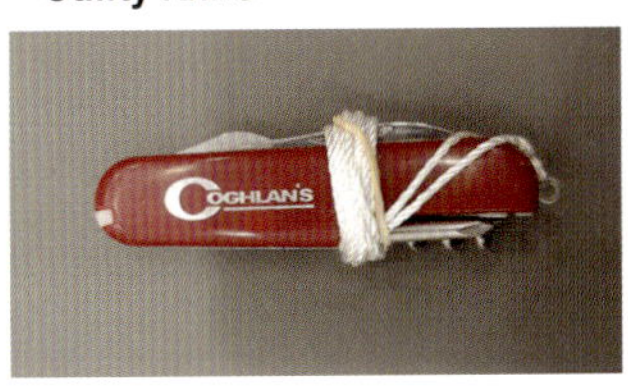

- **Bailing Bucket**

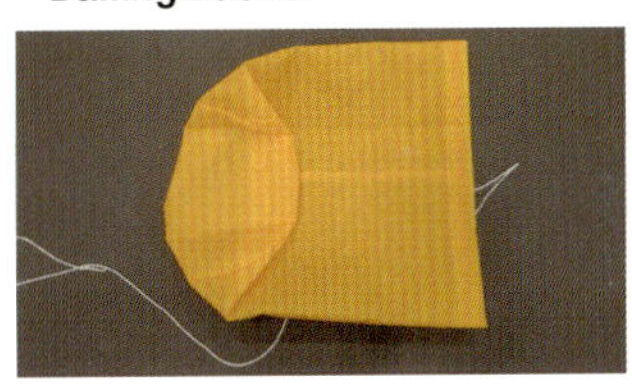

- **Sea Dye Marker**

- **Signal Mirror**

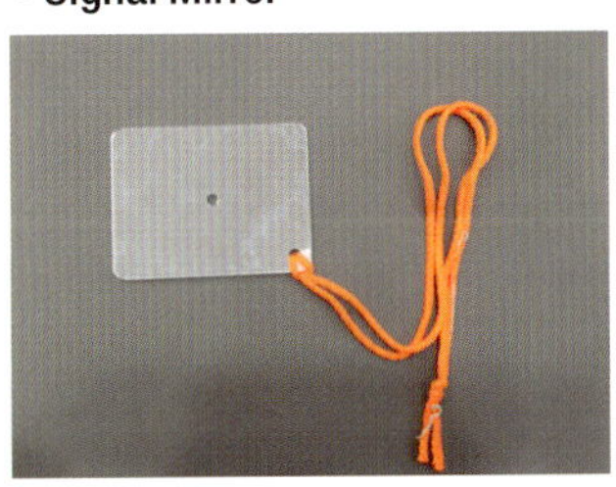

- **Survival Manual**

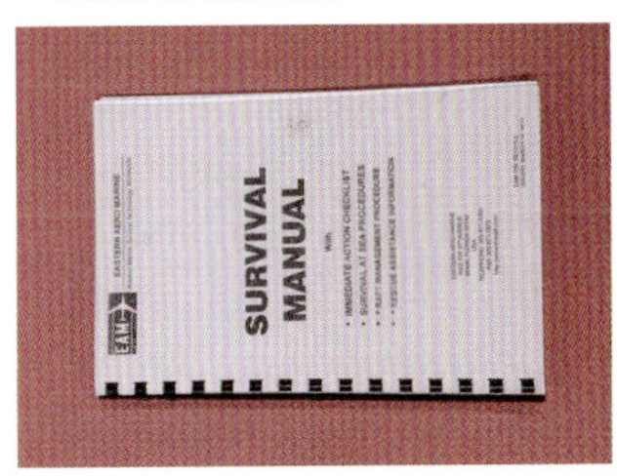

- **Whistle**

- **Flash Light**

- **Pump**

2. Aircraft Security Check

Before flight, under duty purser's instruction, cabin crew shall perform security check according to Aviation Security Regulation. This should be completed before passengers embark and after passengers disembark. Study **check items** on **pre-flight checklist** prior to flight, and check any suspicious items or signs in accordance with the guidelines below. If the check items are sealed, ensure the seals are not tampered. If any suspicious items are found, report to duty purser or captain in order to notify the relevant authorities. Suspicious items: objects threatening aviation security, such as unidentified baggage, boxes, white powder, deadly weapons, etc.

PRE-FLIGHT SECURITY CHECKLIST

(FSR 9.1.20.1)

Date ____________ A/C No HL ____________ A/C TYPE ____________ Flight No. ________

Station (From/To) ________ / ________ Current Alert Level 3(Yellow) □ 2(Orange) □ 1(Red) □

Purser: Name ________________ Signature ________________ Completion Time ______________

PIC: Name ________________ Signature ________________ Completion Time ______________

※ S: Satisfactory U: Unsatisfactory N/A: Not Applicable

Area		Check Items	S	U	N/A
Cabin	Seat	Inside of seat pockets: Alert1 & EU only ***Note 1)**			
		Under the seat cushions and life vests: Alert1 & EU only ** **Note 2)**			
		Upside of seats			
		Both sidewalls including windows			
		Compartments around seats			
		Sidewall stowage bins [A380, 772K, B744 U/D]			
	Aisle	Inside of all overhead bins			
		Corners near the bulkhead and curtain			
		Floor			
	Jump Seat	Crew jumpseats and life vests			
		Emergency equipment storage			
	Door	Corners near the door			
		Inside of coatrooms			
		Inside of magazine racks			
	CRA	Crew rest area [A380, B744, B772, B77WS, A332]			
	VCC	Video control center			
	DFS Area	Duty Free Showcase [A380 Only]			
Lavatory	Facility	Area around the lavatory door, wall and ceiling			
		Area around the toilet			
	Compartment	Towel containers and tissue dispensers			
		Area under sink			
		Rubbish bins			
		Compartments in the back of mirror [A380, B772, B773, B77WS]			
Galley	Compartment	All storage compartments (Ovens, refrigerators, bars)			
		Ceiling, wall and floor			
		Rubbish bins and towel containers			
		Compartments in the ceiling			
		Inside of cart lift (Elevator) [A380, B744]			
	Cart	Carts sealing			

Note 1) 100% Check for Alert Level 1 only. However, 100% Check for FLT departing from EU.

Note 2) 100% Check for Alert Level 1 only. However, 5% Check for FLT departing from EU.

☞ Least Risk Bomb Location and Location of Explosion: The hindmost Door of R Side

Student Activity - **Team Discussion**

Read the case and answer the questions.

You are the cabin crew on the flight bound for New York. After the first meal service, you saw a passenger falling down in front of the L4 lavatory.

Q1. What do you have to do first?

Q2. How do you call for help in the cabin?

Q3. If the passenger is still conscious, then what do you have to do?

Q4. Refer to the First Aid Flow Chart. Write down how you would handle an unconscious passenger.

Chapter 7

During Boarding

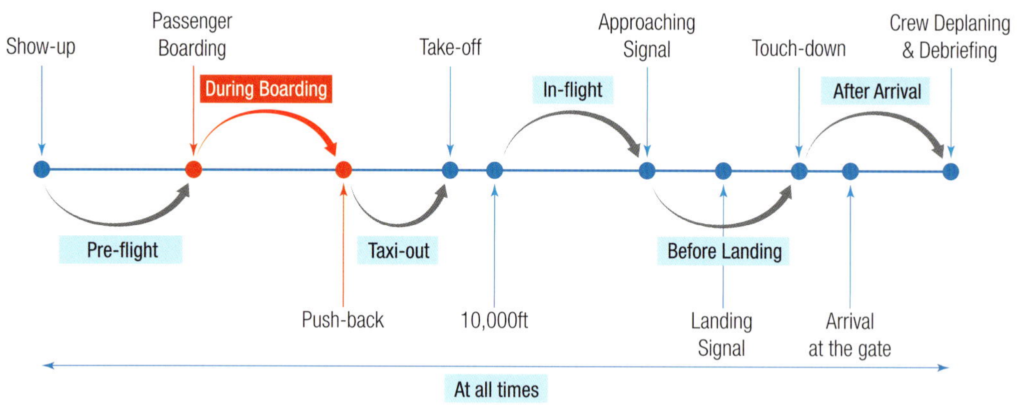

Ⅰ. Cabin Crew Duties for Boarding

During passengers' boarding, cabin crew shall check boarding passes to prevent unauthorized aircraft access. If the person refuses or cannot produce proper identification, try to keep the person under surveillance and notify ground staff or law enforcement. And cabin crew should be evenly distributed throughout the cabin to assist evacuation at any time. Specific duties during passenger boarding should also include:

• Monitoring passenger flow
• Monitoring the exits and aisle(s) to ensure they remain clear of obstructions
• Assisting passengers, especially those requiring special assistance
• Monitoring the size, weight and stowage of cabin baggage
• Observing passengers for signs of sickness, intoxication or unruly behavior

Dmitry Birin / Shutterstock.com

II. Stowage of Carry-on Baggage

Carry-on baggage brought on board must be properly stowed prior to closing the door, taking-off, and landing of the aircraft. Especially, emergency exit seats must be clear in accordance with safety regulations.

• Passenger carry-on baggage should be stored in these spaces:
  - Overhead bin
  - Underneath passenger seat with forward and side restraints
  - Enclosed coatroom (closet)
• Carry-on baggage may not be stowed in any area that interferes with crew access to emergency equipment or blocks passenger view of required signs.
• Non-enclosed coat closets not equipped

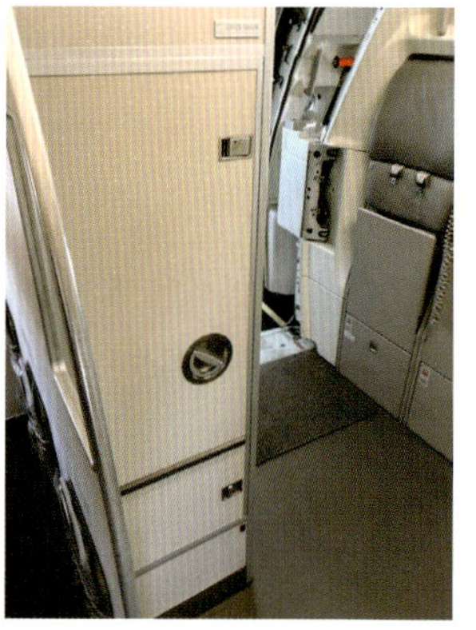

with door, net, safety strap, etc. are for coats and hanging garment bags only. Carry-on baggage may not be stowed on these closet floors.

- No baggage can be stowed at places such as underneath passenger seat without forward restraint and side restraints for aisle seat.
- Carry-on baggage may not be strapped into a seat.
(Cabin reserved seat baggage can be strapped into a seat.)
- No baggage must be stowed in lavatories.
- Weight limitations placarded for each stowage area must be complied.

III. Exit Availability

Any time passengers are on board, at least one floor-level exit must be available for normal or emergency exit. The term 'be available' means a situation with the door in armed position or step car in ready-to-use position. Aircraft surface movement is prohibited unless each door is armed for emergency exit. From surface movement, all exits must be armed and ready for evacuation.

IV. Aircraft Fueling

Fueling or de-fueling while passengers are on board, boarding or deplaning is prohibited.

However, it may be allowed by the captain in accordance with regulations. Cabin crew must be positioned close to each assigned exit, and the boarding bridge or step car must be in place at the open door. 'No Smoking' and 'Exit' sign must be turned on and 'Fasten Seat Belt' sign must be turned off.

Stanislaw Tokarski / Shutterstock.com

V. Carriage of Special Category Passengers

1. Passengers Not Acceptable

Before closing the door, duty purser should advise captain of presence of the following passengers if found. Captain determines whether the concerned passenger is acceptable or not.

- A person who obstructs aircraft operation and safety by committing violence, threats, or violation or tampering doors, exits, or any equipment of aircraft
- A person who appears to be intoxicated or under the influence of drugs
- A person who refuses security check or identification
- A person who damages other passengers or their belongings
- Any other persons who are not acceptable for safe aircraft operation

American Woman Dragged Off Korean Air Flight After Demanding Seat Upgrade in 'Major Disturbance'

(Source: https://www.newsweek.com)

2. Passengers with Reduced Mobility

A passenger with reduced mobility (PRM) is any person whose mobility is reduced due to physical deficiency, intellectual deficiency, age, illness or any other cause of disability, and who needs some degree of assistance. This requirement will become apparent from special requests made by the passenger and/or their family, a medical authority, operator personnel or other industry-associated persons (e.g., travel agents). The level of assistance required from the airport and/or the operator can vary depending on the needs of the individual PRM when traveling by air.

Passengers with Reduced Mobility

Code	Description
BLND	Blind passenger – specify if accompanied by seeing-eye dog or other service animal
DEAF	Deaf passenger – specify if accompanied by a service animal
WCHR	Wheelchair – Ramp – passenger can ascend/descend steps and make his/her own way to/from cabin seat, but requires wheelchair for distance to/from aircraft (i.e., across ramp, finger dock or to mobile lounge, as applicable).
WCHS	Wheelchair – Steps – passenger cannot ascend/descend steps, but is able to make own way to/from cabin seat; requires wheelchair for distance to/from aircraft or mobile lounge and must be carried up/down steps.
WCHC	Wheelchair – Cabin Seat – passenger completely confined to wheelchair; requires wheelchair to/from aircraft/mobile lounge and must be carried up/down steps and to/from cabin seat by trained personnel.
MEDA	Medical case – company medical clearance may be required. Generally not to be used for PRMs who only require special assistance or handling. However, depending on the reason for reduced mobility, it may be necessary to have a medical clearance.
OXYG	Oxygen – for passengers traveling seated or on a stretcher needing oxygen during the flight
STCR	Stretcher passenger

3. Incapacitated Passengers

A completed Medical Information Form (MEDIF) or equivalent is required for passengers who:

- May be suffering from any disease that is believed to be actively contagious and communicable
- Could be considered to be a potential hazard to the safety or punctuality of the flight (including the possibility of diversion and unscheduled landing of the flight)
- Would require medical attention and/or special equipment to maintain their health during the flight
- Might have their medical condition aggravated during, or because of, the flight

Medical Information Form

Dear Doctor,

Airline travel has some unique features that must be considered for certain passengers, so please note the following information before filling out the form.

a. Reduced oxygen pressure: The ambient partial pressure of oxygen in flight is 25 - 30% lower than on the ground. If a passenger has heart/lung disease or anemia, supplemental oxygen may be required during flight.

b. Reduced atmospheric pressure: Cabin air pressure changes greatly during take-off and landing and expansion and contraction of gas in body cavities can cause pain and affect surgical suture sites.

c. Turbulence: Spinal disease can be worsened by sudden turbulence and impact from landing.

d. Absence of advanced medical care: Please be advised that cabin attendants cannot provide special assistance to patient passengers. Also, they are only trained for first aid and are not permitted to give medication or administer any injection.

e. Increased risk of deep vein thrombosis: Please consider DVT (Deep Vein Thrombosis) prophylaxis for any passenger who is elderly, has a history of cancer, had recent surgery (major hip, knee, or ankle) or trauma as sitting immobilized in a cramped seat may increase the risk of deep vein thrombosis.

For further information, please refer to the IATA Medical Manual.

IATA

Medical Manual
Appendix 'E'

Attachment A

Information sheet for passengers requiring special assistance

1. Family name First name Title
2. Passenger name record (PNR)
3. Proposed itinerary From (Airport) To (Airport)
   Airline(s) Flight #(s) Class(es)
   Date(s) yyyy/mm/dd Segment(s)
4. Nature of illness
5. Intended escorts ◯ Yes No Name Title Age
   PNR if different Medical qualification ◯ Yes No Language spoken
6. Wheelchair required ◯ Yes No Specify wheelchair categories (please select)
   Passenger own wheelchair ◯ Yes No Specify wheelchair type (please select) Weight & size Specify Metric or imperial (e.g. Kg or Lbs, etc.)
7. Ambulance needed (to be arranged by the passenger or his/her representative) Yes ◯ No
   If yes, specify name of ambulance company
   Name of contact Contact tel. no.
8. Meet and assist (if available) ◯ Yes No If designated person, specify contact
9. Other ground arrangements needed ◯ Yes No
   If yes, specify
   Departure airport Transit airport Arrival airport
10. Special in-flight arrangements needed ◯ Yes No
    If yes, specify:
    Stretcher ◯ Yes No
    If yes, specify arranging company
    specify at whose expense
    Oxygen ◯ Yes No If yes, specify* (please select)
    Does the passenger needs to travel with an emotional support animal? Yes No If yes, specify
    Special equipment provided by the passenger ◯ Yes No If yes, specify (please select) ☐ equipment is autonomous
    Special meals ◯ Yes No If yes, specify (please select)
    Special seating arrangement ◯ Yes No If yes, specify (please select)
    NOTE: EXIT ROW CANNOT BE USED BY DISABLED/ILL PASSENGERS BECAUSE OF SAFETY REGULATIONS
11. Frequent traveler medical clearance (FREMEC) for this airline ◯ Yes No
    If yes, specify FREMEC number issued by expiry date

** Be advised that some aircraft may be limited in the oxygen flow rate available and that the oxygen may be offered with 'pulsed' flow.*

2017-08

Source: IATA, Medical Report (June 2018), Appendix 'E', page 77

4. Infants

Infants (at least 7 days but younger than 2 years) are accepted for travel on international/domestic flights. Any infant will be accepted without restriction as long as he/she is accompanied by an adult and not suffering from any illness. Passengers with an infant may not sit in an exit row seat.

Seating Restrictions and Guidelines

Life Vest

The total number of passengers should not exceed the numbers of loaded life vests (for use in emergency ditching) in each flight. If the total number of passengers is more than the number of loaded life vests, report to the Captain and ask for the additional life vests. Life vests for infants may, upon request, be provided for passengers traveling with infants and it should be collected and stored in an appropriate place after flight.

Oxygen Mask

Airlines assign seats considering the number of passengers including infants and the number of provided oxygen masks. Cabin crew should ensure that the number of infants do not exceed the number of oxygen masks in the set of seats.

5. UM: Unaccompanied Minor

UM means a child passenger (5 - 12 years old) who is traveling by himself/herself. The operator is responsible for the safe delivery of UMs to the receiving guardian at the transfer station or final destination. It is recommended that operators use a form to track the movement of each UM in its care. The form should be completed at each relevant point of the UM journey when transferring responsibility to others.

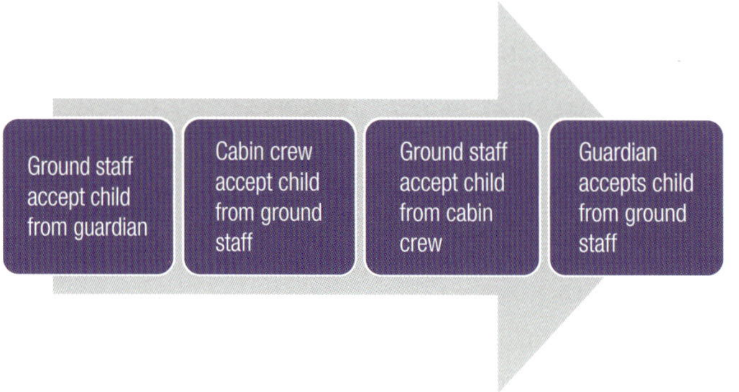

Source: IATA, Cabin Operations Safety – Best Practices Guide 3rd edition(2017), page 88

The duty purser will receive the UM envelope containing the passport and entry documents for the destination country from the ground staff. The duty purser will hand over UM and the UM envelope containing the passport and entry documents for the destination country to the ground staff at destination.

Hispanolistic /iStock

6. Deportee, Inadmissible Passenger

Deportee (DEPO) is a person who involuntarily receives a deportation order from the authorities of the country. Inadmissible Passenger (INAD) is a person whose entry or transit is rejected by reason of disqualification for entry such as no visa, expiry of passport, an attempt to enter contrary to the visa and so on.

Handling Procedure of DEPO & INAD

The station manager of the deporting station notifies boarding of deportee passengers to the duty purser and relays the following documents:

- DEPO's passport
- Official document of deportation order by the authorities (if possible)
- DEPO's name and SHR with the name and Seat No.
- Credit Agreement & Invoice Copy
  (In case the airline pays for the returning ticket)
- Duty purser must not hand over, in any case, any documents from a deporting station to the DEPO passenger in aircraft. All documents, as well as the DEPO passenger, must be relayed to the ground staff at the destination.

7. Passengers in Custody

A passenger in custody should be escorted throughout the trip by two or more police officers. However, when the flight time is less than 4 hours and the prisoner is not a violent criminal, one escort is possible. Escorts should be equipped with adequate restraining devices to be used in the event they determine that restraint is necessary. Under normal circumstances, a prisoner should not be shackled to any part of the aircraft, including seats, tables, etc. Escorting officer and the prisoner should be accompanied at all times and kept under surveillance. Neither the prisoner nor officers should be served alcoholic beverages, and metal cutlery should not be given to the prisoner.

VI. Exit Row Seating Regulations

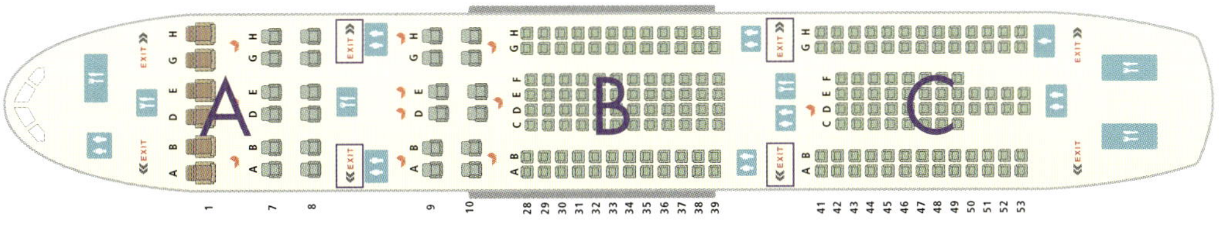

Exit row seats are those seats **having direct access** to an exit, and those seats in a row of seats through which passengers would have to pass to gain access to an exit. A passenger seat having 'direct access' means a seat from which a passenger can proceed directly to the exit without entering an aisle or passing around an obstruction.

1. Cabin Crew Duties Regarding Exit Row Seating

Cabin crew must visually assess passengers seated in the exit row seats to determine suitability during passenger boarding and before landing. When briefing the passengers seated in the exit row seats, cabin crew must tell them about the safety information card and how to operate the exit.

2. A Passenger May Not Sit in an Exit Row Seat If:

- The person **lacks sufficient strength, mobility or dexterity** in both arms, hands and both legs so that he or she may have difficulties to operate the exit and help other passengers to evacuate.
- The person lacks **sufficient visual capacity** to perform the above functions without the assistance of visual aids beyond contact lenses or eye glasses.
- The person lacks **sufficient aural capacity** to hear and understand instructions shouted by cabin crew without assistance other than a hearing aid.
- The person lacks the ability adequately to impart information orally to other passengers.
- The person is **less than 15 years** of age or lacks the capacity to perform one or more of the applicable functions listed above without the assistance of an adult companion.

3. Exit Row Seat Passenger Duties

- Assess conditions outside an exit to ensure safe evacuation.
- Locate and operate an emergency exit.
- Follow oral instructions and/or hand signals given by a crew member.
- Open and stow or secure an emergency exit so it will not interfere with passengers exiting the aircraft.
- Assess the condition of, activate, and stabilize an escape slide to assist others in evacuating.
- Pass expeditiously through an emergency exit and follow a safe path away from the exit.

Exit Row Seat Passenger Briefing

안녕하십니까? 이곳은 비상구 열 좌석으로 비상시 승무원을 도와주셔야 합니다. 협조해 주시겠습니까? 비상구 좌석 승객의 임무는 비상구 외부 상황을 확인하고 승무원의 지시 및 신호에 따르는 것입니다. 비상구는 항공기 외부에 이상이 없고 승무원의 요청이 있는 경우에만 개방할 수 있습니다. 탈출 전 미끄럼대 상태를 확인 후, 먼저 탈출하시고 이후 내려오는 승객들을 도와주며 항공기로부터 대피하도록 안내해 주십시오.
감사합니다.

You are seated in an exit seat and you should help cabin crew in an emergency situation. Would you help us in the event of emergency?
Passengers seated in an emergency exit seat should assess the conditions outside of the exit and follow signals given by crew members. When the emergency exit is free of externally hazardous objects, open the emergency exit according to the instructions of crew members. Please assess the condition of the slide, and be the first to evacuate. Then assist others in evacuating and direct the evacuees away from the aircraft.

Student Activity - **Team Discussion**

Watch the video, read the article, and answer the questions.

Video: https://youtu.be/FRYy9L9jzyA
Article: https://www.nbcbayarea.com

Q1. **Where was the passenger – Benjamin Levy – seated in the flight?**

Q2. **What were the actions Mr. Benjamin Levy took at the time of the aircraft crash?**

Q3. **Let's assume that you are a cabin crew in the flight. Do the exit briefing to the passengers seated in the exit seat.**

Chapter

8

Before Push-back, During Taxi-Out, and Before Take-off

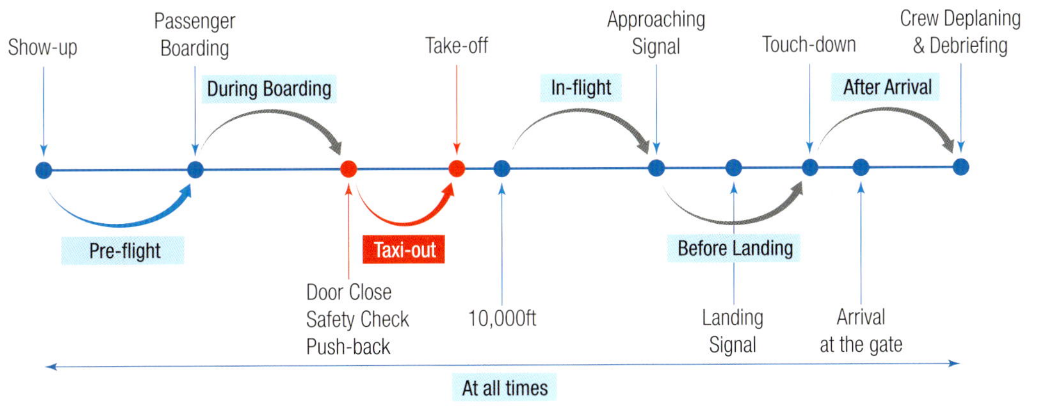

I. Before Push-back: Preparation for Aircraft Movement

1. Cabin is Ready for Closing Door

The closing of the entry door by the duty purser (after communication and coordination with the flight crew) usually indicates to the flight crew that the cabin is ready for push-back. Prior to closing door, the duty purser verbally confirms to the captain ("Captain, we have 000 passengers, 00 extra crew (if applicable) on board. We are ready to close the door.").

And the followings should usually be completed before the door is closed:

- Completion of all passengers' boarding
- All carry-on baggage properly stowed
- Overhead bins closed

2. Door Mode Change: Preparation of Doors for Push-back

The **door mode change** is conducted to ensure that the door is ready for emergency evacuation or passenger deplaning. Door mode change should be made by duty purser's PA command (e. g. "Cabin crew door side standby and safety check!") and cabin crew members respond to purser's all attendant call.

3. The Safety Check: Cabin is Ready for Push-back

Push-back is pushing an airplane backwards away from an airport gate by external power, which is a low-profile vehicle called a tug-car. The captain shall not initiate an aircraft push-back unless the duty purser advises "Cabin is ready for push-back". The duty purser verbally confirms "Cabin is ready for push-back" signifying the safety check. The **safety check** is conducted to ensure that the cabin is completely ready for push-back. To respond to the **all attendant call** before surface movement is to report that the following are cleared as well as that the door mode is changed.

- Cabin is ready for closing door.
- Emergency equipment has been checked (if not already notified).

- Exit row seats have been assessed.
- Service carts are properly stowed.
- All passengers are seated with seat belts securely fastened.
- In-seat videos, tray tables and footrests (except EY/CL) are properly stowed and seatbacks are in upright position.
- All doors are armed, cross-checked and properly closed.

II. During Taxi-Out

1. Sterile Cockpit

The purpose of a sterile cockpit regulation is to mitigate the risks of flight crew errors being made due to distraction or disturbance at times when full attention to the operation of the aircraft is required. The concept is such that cabin crew should not contact or interrupt the flight crew in any way during the critical phases of flight. The critical phases of flight usually include:

- Taxi
- Take-off
- Initial climb (approx. 10 minutes after take-off)
- Approach (approx. 10 minutes prior to landing)
- Any other phases of flight below 10,000 feet
- Landing

Cabin crew can tell the beginning and the termination of **critical phases of flight** by checking the **on/off** of the 'Fasten Seat Belt' sign and standard communication signals during take-off and landing. Procedures for a sterile cockpit during critical phases of flight usually allow a procedure for communication between the cabin crew and flight crew in the event of an emergency.

Critical 11 Minutes

'Critical 11 Minutes' refers to the three minutes after take-off and the eight minutes before landing when the cabin crew is prohibited from attempting to communicate with the cockpit except on matters critical to the safety of the flight and passengers, and the cockpit crew is required to refrain from any activity not associated with control of the aircraft. This practice stems from the fact that 80 percent of accidents involving commercial aircraft occur within these two periods when an aircraft is most vulnerable to many dangers.

2. Cabin Crew Surface Movement Regulations

To help mitigate the risk of injury to cabin crew while the aircraft is moving on the ground, cabin crew should be seated in their assigned crew seats except while performing safety-related duties such as the safety demonstration and securing the cabin for departure. All cabin crew are seated as soon as safety duties are completed. When seated on jumpseats, cabin crew should assume **ready position** like below to protect their body from any impact.

- Secure the seat belt low and tight and shoulder harness across body.
- Sit upright and well back on the jumpseat and place feet flat on floor.
- Sit on hands, palms up.
- Cabin crew should conduct **30 second review** to maintain emergency preparedness.

30 Second Review

The objective of the **30 second review** (also called **silent review**) is to mentally prepare cabin crew for any eventualities that may occur during take-off and landing, so that they are prepared for unexpected emergency situations.

- Emergency equipment location and operation
- Exit location and operation
- Emergency procedures
- Bracing commands
- Passengers who could assist in an emergency
- Passengers who may need assistance in an emergency

3. Passenger Briefing

Cabin crew should give a passenger briefing with contents below during taxi-out on every flight even on a flight with no new passengers. The following are the contents of a passenger briefing:

- Emergency exits, seat belt, oxygen mask, life vest, and other emergency equipment
- Contents of safety information card in each passengers' seat pocket
- Other useful information (such as smoking restrictions)

Passenger Briefing Announcement

계속해서 이 비행기의 비상구 위치와 비상장비 사용법에 대해 안내해 드리겠습니다.
잠시 주목해 주시기 바랍니다.
Ladies and gentlemen. We will now show you the safety features of this aircraft. Please give your full attention for a few minutes.

이 비행기의 비상구는 모두 여덟 개로 좌, 우에 각각 있습니다.
There are 8 emergency exits on both sides of the aircraft.

비상시 비행기의 전원이 꺼질 경우 비상구까지 유도 등이 통로에 켜지게 됩니다.
If there is loss of power in an emergency, emergency track lights will turn on and guide you to the exit.

좌석벨트 사인이 켜지면, 좌석벨트를 매 주십시오.
When the seat belt sign is on, please fasten your seat belt.

벨트는 버클을 끼워 허리 아래로 내려서 조여 주시고 풀 때는 덮개를 들어올리면 됩니다.
To fasten the seat belt, insert the link into the main buckle and tighten the strap across your hips securely. To release the seat belt, raise the flap of the buckle.

산소마스크는 선반 속에 있으며 산소 공급이 필요한 비상시에 저절로 내려옵니다.
Your oxygen mask is in the overhead compartment, and it will drop automatically when needed.

마스크가 내려오면 앞으로 잡아 당겨 코와 입에 대시고 끈으로 머리에 고정해 주십시오.
When the mask appears, pull the mask towards you and cover your nose and mouth, then adjust the elastic head band.

도움이 필요한 동반자가 있을 때는 먼저 착용하신 후 도와주시기 바랍니다.
Please put your mask on first, and then help somebody who may need your assistance.

여러분의 좌석(또는 팔걸이) 아래에 있는 구명복은 비행기가 바다에 내렸을 경우 사용하시게 됩니다.
Your life vest is located under your seat (or besides your seat).

착용하실 때는 머리 위에서부터 입으시고, 버클을 끼운 다음 몸에 맞도록 조절해 주십시오.
To put the vest on, slip it over your head, then adjust the strap around your waist.

구명복은 기내에서 부풀지 않도록 유의해 주시고 부풀릴 때는 탈출 직전 비상구 앞에서 붉은색 손잡이를 당기시면 됩니다.
To inflate the vest, pull the red tabs down in front of an exit door just before leaving the aircraft.

충분히 부풀지 않을 때는 양쪽의 고무관을 힘껏 불어주십시오
You can also inflate it by blowing into the tubes.

보다 자세한 사항은 앞 좌석 주머니 속에 있는 안내문을 참고하시기 바랍니다.
For further information, please refer to the safety information card in your seat pocket.

아울러 안내문에 설명된 바와 같이 항공기내에서의 흡연은 엄격히 금지되어 있음을 알려 드립니다.
Also, we'd like to remind you smoking is strictly prohibited during the flight.

감사합니다.

III. Before Take-off

1. Cabin Secure Check: Cabin is Ready for Take-off

When captain gives a **take-off** signal, purser should conduct the final cabin checks like below, and gives a call to captain **"Cabin is ready for take-off"**.

- Cabin is ready for push-back.
- Passenger safety briefing is conducted.
- Movable items in cabin/galleys are stowed.
- All cabin crew are seated with seat belt and shoulder harness fastened.
- When the take-off signal is on, duty purser verbally confirms "Cabin is ready for take-off", signifying the above. Captain must not initiate an aircraft take-off unless duty purser advises.

2. Rejected Take-off

Rejected take-off refers to any take-off that has been discontinued on runway after take-off roll has begun in the event of an engine malfunction, the recognition of a significant abnormality, or an ATC instruction to stop the aircraft during the take-off roll. The decision to do so is made at a speed not greater than the correctly calculated decision speed (V1). After V1, a reject should only be considered if there is a strong reason to believe that the aircraft will not fly .

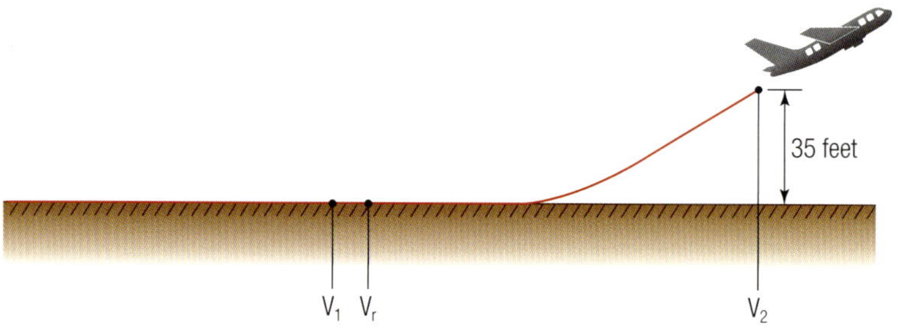

Cabin crew should evaluate the situation according to captain's PA and respond appropriately. When rejected take-off occurs, PIC will make the following announcement, "This is the captain, remain seated, remain seated." Cabin crew should stay at the right position for the next steps.

Student Activity - **Team Discussion**

Scan the QR code to watch the video and answer the questions.

(Source: https://youtu.be/8lSbPWn_6R4)

Q1. What do you remember about the safety related information that is shown in the video?

Q2. Korean Air has recently launched new passenger safety cabin video. It has been controversial that the video is lack of delivering safety information to passengers, only focused on entertaining. What are your opinions about this issue? Discuss with your team members.

Q3. Many passengers don't pay attention to the cabin safety video. How can airlines effectively deliver safety information to passengers? Make your own safety video with your team members. You may refer to the safety videos of other airlines on YouTube.

Chapter

9

In-flight, Before Landing, and After Arrival

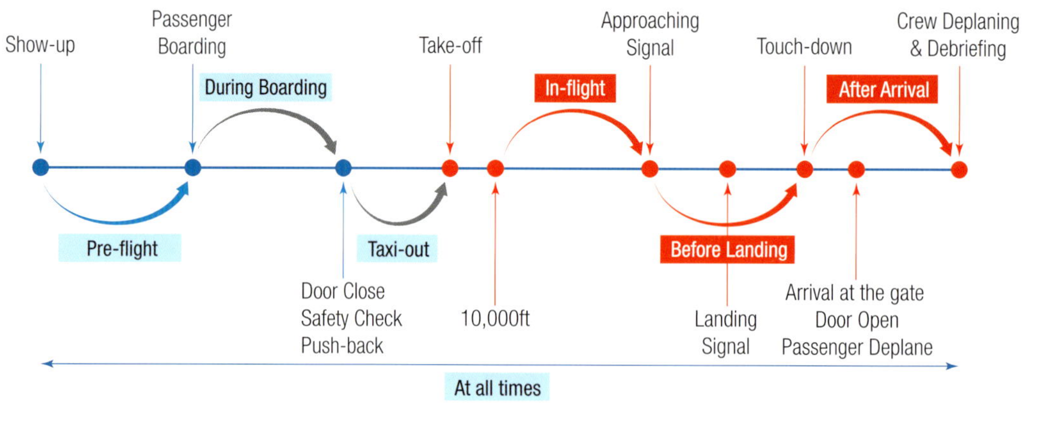

I. In-flight

1. Turbulence Guidelines

Turbulence is a sudden, violent shift in airflow caused by wind, storms, jet stream, and objects near the plane. Sudden turbulence can cause injury to passengers and cabin crew. So, the flight crew should proactively communicate turbulence advisories to the cabin crew and passengers using the interphone, PA system and 'Fasten Seat Belt' signs. The captain should provide the duty purser with the estimated time, level and duration of turbulence before encountering each one if possible as it may take several minutes to secure the cabin (discontinue service, stow the cart etc. if necessary). Cabin crew should make sure all passengers should keep their seat belts fastened at all times during the flight.

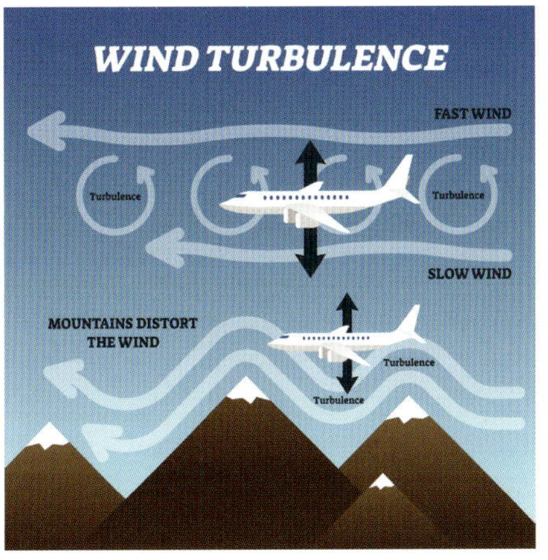

Turbulence Level and How to Respond When Encountering Turbulence

Light Turbulence	Moderate Turbulence	Severe Turbulence
• Perform safety and seat belt compliance checks. • Continue service with caution. • Consider suspension of hot beverage service.	• Suspend service. • Perform safety and seat belt compliance checks, if safe to do so. • Secure in crew seats.	• Suspend service. • Take immediate action to protect individual safety. • If possible, sit in nearest available seat and fasten seat belt/harness. • Assist passengers when safe to do so.

2. Serving Alcohol

Serving alcoholic beverages should be carried out in a responsible manner. This should include tactfully refusing to serve passengers alcoholic beverages when they are displaying signs of intoxication.

Here are the indications of intoxication.

- Loud and slurred speech
- Abnormal stance
- Strong alcohol smell in breath
- Disturbing comfort of other passengers around
- Challenging the crew in the conduct of their duties

Alcoholic beverages shall also not be served to any escorted passenger or her/his escort and anyone under 19 years in age.

II. Before Landing

1. Approaching Procedures

When **approaching signal is on**, duty purser rechecks the cabin readiness as following.

- Ensure that carry-on baggage is stowed in a proper manner.
- Collect cups and glasses.
- Ensure that galley and associated equipment is stowed.

2. Landing Procedure

When **landing signal is on**, duty purser rechecks the cabin readiness as follows and contacts captain if it is considered impossible to get ready by landing time.

- Cabin is secure and ready for landing.
- All passengers are seated with seat belts securely fastened.
- Seatbacks are in upright position.
- Tray tables, footrests (except EY/CL) and personal monitors are properly stowed.

3. Cabin Crew Seated for Landing

To help mitigate the risk of injury to cabin crew members, cabin crew must be seated for landing as soon as all safety-related duties and checks have been completed and should remain seated until parked at the gate, except to perform safety-related duties such as disarming doors or responding to an abnormal or emergency situation.

III. After Arrival

1. Preparation of Doors for Arrival

Cabin crew should change the door mode from **arming** to **disarming** upon the duty purser's PA command.

2. Door Operation

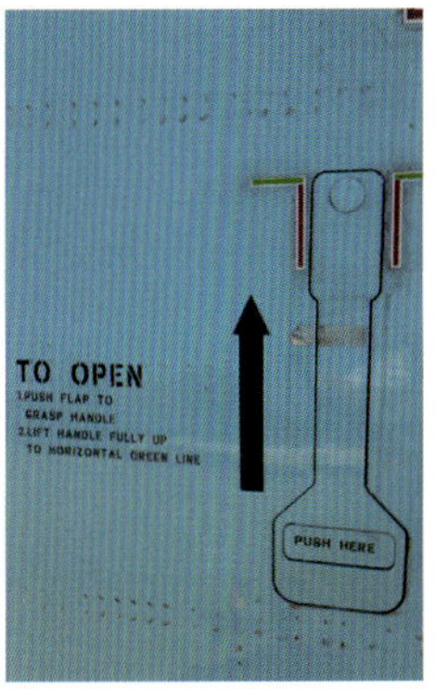

In order to prevent injury to personnel and damage to aircraft and equipment due to misinterpretation, only standard signals should be used to indicate to the cabin crew responsible for the door operation that the ground equipment such as step car or passenger boarding bridge is correctly positioned.

The standard signals usually used for these purposes are:

- Ground staff knocks at the door.
- Crew members give a thumbs-up signal when the door is ready for opening.

3. Passenger Deplaning

Viktor Konya / Shutterstock.com

During the disembarkation process, the risk of an evacuation remains. Cabin crew should, therefore, remain alert to outside and inside conditions and remain available at the door area(s) to perform an evacuation should it become necessary.

4. Security Check

Cabin crew shall check to see if there are any item left behind or remaining passengers after each flight operation and also prevent unauthorized/unidentified persons and articles from having access to aircraft.

Student Activity - **Team Discussion**

Scan the QR code to watch the video and answer the questions.

(Source: https://youtu.be/_w6OnK-Djns)

Q1. What is the common cause of turbulence?

Q2. What is thermal turbulence and how is it created?

Q3. What is mechanical turbulence and how is it created?

Student Activity - Part II Practical Evaluation

1. Emergency Equipment Drill

Emergency Equipment				
Subject	Contents	1	2	3
Flashlight	Pre-Flight Check			
	Usage			
PO_2 Bottle	Pre-Flight Check			
	Usage			
PBE	Pre-Flight Check			
	Usage			
Halon Extinguisher	Pre-Flight Check			
	Usage			
H_2O Extinguisher	Pre-Flight Check			
	Usage			
Megaphone	Pre-Flight Check			
	Usage			
FAK	Pre-Flight Check			
	Usage			
EMK	Pre-Flight Check			
	Usage			
AED	Pre-Flight Check			
	Usage			

2. Safety Demonstration Drill

Safety Demonstration				
Subject	Contents	1	2	3
Exit Briefing	Present Exit Briefing			
Manual Demo	Present Manual Safety Demonstration			
CPR	Perform the CPR			

PART

3

Managing Emergency Situations

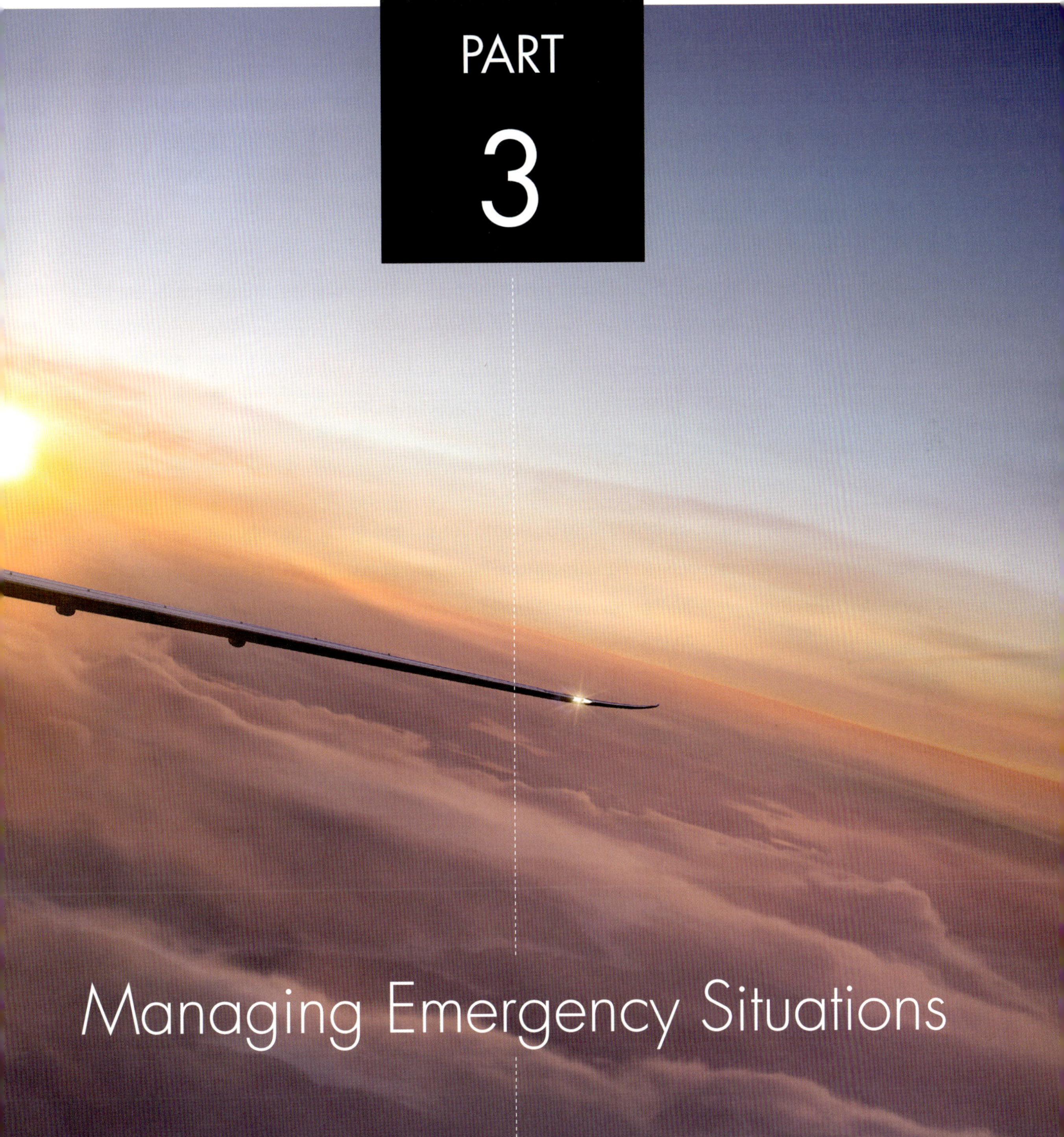

The Convention on International Civil Aviation Annex 13 defines an aviation accident as "an occurrence associated with the operation of an aircraft, which takes place between the time any person boards the aircraft and until all such persons have disembarked, where a person is fatally or seriously injured, the aircraft sustains damage or structural failure, or the aircraft is missing or is completely inaccessible." And Annex 13 further defines an aviation incident as "an occurrence, other than an accident, associated with the operation of an aircraft which affects or could affect the safety of operation."

Common examples of aircraft accidents are cabin fire, decompression, aircraft crash, etc. When an aircraft accident or incident occurs, an emergency evacuation may be required for the safety of passengers and crew members. Aviation accidents and incidents may occur at any time during the flight; to minimizc harmful effects of such event, cabin crew must be well trained to respond such events.

In PART 3, first we will look into how to deal with smoke and fire in the cabin, and we will also look into the decompression handling procedures, and at last, we will study emergency evacuation handling procedures which are cabin crew's most important safety related duties.

Chapter 10

Smoke, Fumes and Fire

I. Basic Concept of Fire

1. Three Elements of Fire

The three elements of fire are oxygen, heat and fuel. To extinguish the fire, we just need to remove one of three elements of fire.

2. Classification of Fire

Fires are classified into three categories, which are A, B, and C, based on what is the fuel of the fire.

• **Class A**

H_2O/Halon
Solid Material

• **Class B**

Halon
Grease

• **Class C**

Halon
Electrical

Class A fire is caused by wood, paper, cloth or other solid material. It can be extinguished by both H_2O and halon type extinguisher. Class B fire is caused by flammable liquids such as oil, gasoline, alcohol, paint. It cannot be extinguished by H_2O type extinguisher, and could be more dangerous when using H_2O type extinguisher. Therefore, to extinguish Class B fire, only halon extinguisher is used. Class C fire is caused by electrical outlets, power poles, high voltage lines, and other electrical equipment. To extinguish the Class C fire, you should use halon extinguisher. If you use H_2O type extinguisher, there is a risk of electric shock.

3. Fire-fighting Equipment in the Cabin

• H_2O Extinguisher

• Halon Extinguisher

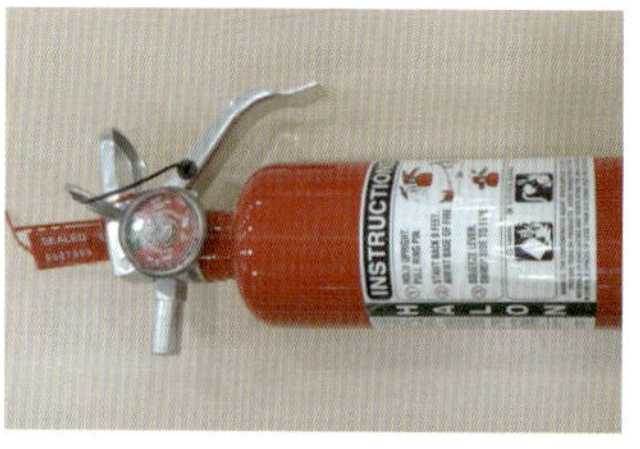

• Heat Activated Halon Extinguisher

• PBE (Protective Breathing Equipment)

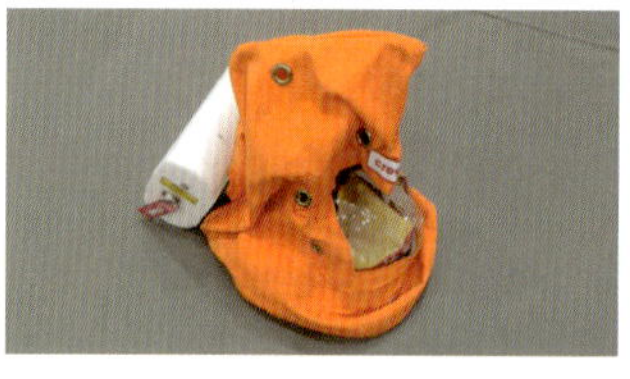

• Fireproof Glove

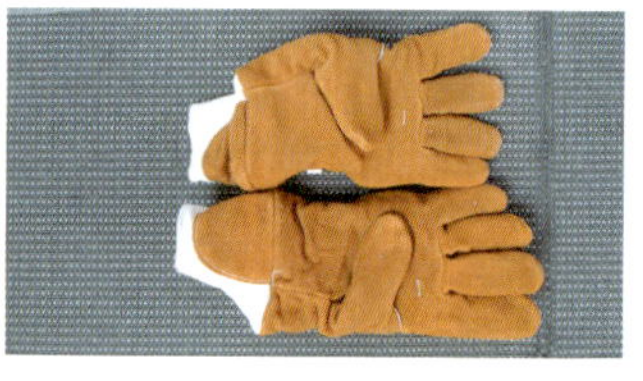

• Crash Axe

• Emergency Power-off Switch

• Circuit Breaker

• Smoke Detector

II. Cabin Crew Response to Smoke, Fumes and Fire

1. Call for Help

- Cabin crew who discovers the potential smoke, fumes, and fire first should inform other cabin crew.

- One cabin crew must establish and maintain communication with the cockpit and describe the smoke, fumes, and fire including:
  - Exact location (lavatory, air vents, overhead bins, lower side wall, oven, etc.)
  - Texture (dense, billowing, rolling, thick, wispy, thin, etc.)
  - Color (gray, black, white, blue, brown, etc.)
  - Odor (putrid, electrical, rubbery, oily, etc.)

2. Locate Source of Smoke, Fumes, and Fire

- Thoroughly inspect the source of fire.
- If the source is not visible or readily accessible, inform the captain.
- Remove any PO_2 bottles out of the area of smoke and fire.

3. Determine Classification of Fire and Appropriate Fire Extinguisher

- Do not delay fighting the fire if the classification of the fire is not clear.
- When in doubt, use the halon extinguisher and then follow up with the H_2O extinguisher if appropriate.

4. Cut the Power Source, If Applicable

- Turn off the equipment.
- Pull corresponding circuit breakers.
- Lift the protective cover and position the **emergency power off switch** to **off** (only applicable to aircraft equipped with emergency power off switch).

5. Fight the Fire

- Fight the **fire**, **not** the **smoke** and **fumes**.
- Obtain and don **PBE**, if necessary.
- Wear **fireproof gloves**, if necessary.
- Thoroughly inspect the source of fire to ensure it is extinguished.

6. Spray Extinguisher on Hot Surface to Ensure the Fire is Out

- Gather additional equipment to fight the fire.
- Cabin crews who are not communicating with the captain or locating and fighting the fire should gather extinguishers and PBEs and make them available to the crews fighting the fire.
- A cabin crew gathering the equipment may need to don the PBE and take over fighting the fire.

7. Care for Passengers

- Move passengers away from smoke, fumes, or fire.
- Use the PA or megaphone to communicate with passengers.
- In a smoke or fumes-filled cabin:
  - Advise passengers to keep heads at armrest level.
  - If applicable, distribute wet towels for passengers to place over nose and mouth to aid in breathing.

III. Cabin Crew Response in Case of Lavatory Fires

If a smoke detector sounds or there is smoke or other evidence of a lavatory fire, respond as follows:

1. If Lavatory is Occupied

- If lavatory is occupied, attempt to communicate with the passenger inside.
- If cigarette smoke is the cause of the smoke detector sounding, have the passenger extinguish the cigarette.
- After confirming the cigarette is completely extinguished, cabin crew should silence the alarm by clearing the smoke from the lavatory through the open door.
- Warn the passenger that smoking on the airplane can be punished by the aviation law.
- Report to captain. Share the information with other crew members and keep continued watch on it.

Brooks Kraft LLC/Corbis via Getty Images

2. If Lavatory is Not Occupied

- If lavatory is not occupied, feel the door for heat with the back of your hands to find the location of the fire.
- Initiate 'Cabin Crew Response to Smoke, Fumes and Fire'.
- Quickly prepare for the fire-fighting equipment with the door closed.
- Open lavatory door carefully.

- Spray Halon type extinguisher through the door.
- If material in the waste bin is burning, open the waste disposal door and discharge Halon directly into the waste bin. When the fire is out, use a H_2O extinguisher to extinguish any burning material and prevent re-ignition.
- When fire is successfully extinguished, advise the captain and lock the lavatory.

IV. In Case of Oven Fires

In addition to the basic firefighting procedures outlined under 'Cabin Crew Response to Smoke, Fumes and Fire', follow the guidelines below for oven fires.

- Keep oven door closed to deplete the oxygen and smother the fire.
- Pull circuit breaker or position the **emergency power off switch** to **off** (only applicable to aircraft equipped with emergency power off switch).

Marina Lystseva/ASS via Getty Images

Student Activity - **Team Discussion**

Read the article and answer the questions.

Plane crashes that changed aviation

(Source: https://maydaytvshow.fandom.com/wiki/Air_Canada_Flight_797)

Q1. After this accident, the NTSB(National Transportation Safety Board) issued several recommendations to the FAA(Federal Aviation Administration). What are the recommendations about?

Q2. Find out the detailed information of the accident. If you were a cabin crew on the flight, what would you do? Discuss with your team members.

Chapter

11

Decompression

"Communication and coordination among crew members is essential."

I. Types of Decompression

Steve Murphy/AFP via Getty Images

1. Slow Decompression

- A slow decompression is a slow loss of cabin pressure.
- It may be caused by a leak in the seal around a door or window or a malfunctioning pressurization system.

2. Rapid Decompression

- A rapid decompression is a rapid loss of cabin pressure.
- It may be caused by metal fatigue, a bomb explosion, or a weapon firing which breaks the seal.
- In extreme circumstances, a rapid decompression may be categorized as an explosive decompression.

II. Signs of Decompression

1. Common Signs of Every Decompression in the Cabin

• Oxygen masks drop

• Decompression announcements

- "비상 강하 중!"

(**"Attention, emergency descent!"**)

- "벨트를 매고 마스크를 코와 입에 대십시오!"

(**"Fasten your seat belt and put the mask over your nose and mouth!"**)

• 'No Smoking' sign and 'Fasten Seat Belt' sign **on**

2. Some Signs of a Slow Decompression

• Discomfort in the ears

• Whistling sounds

3. Some Signs of a Rapid or Explosive Decompression

• Loud noise and drop in cabin temperature

• Rush of cold air through the cabin

• Sudden fogging of the cabin

• Possible dust, flying debris, ear blockage, ear popping

III. Response to a Decompression

1. Sit down. If a vacant seat is not available, sit on an armrest and/or stabilize yourself wherever you are.
2. Don the nearest oxygen mask.
3. Yell instructions for passengers to do the same.
   - "마스크를 당겨 쓰세요! 벨트 매세요!"

   ("Put on the mask! Fasten your seat belt!")
4. Check if passengers put on the masks while stabilizing yourself.

5. Instruct passengers with eyeglasses to remove them.
6. Instruct an adult who already has a mask on to assist a child.
7. Instruct guardians traveling with a child to don their mask first and then assist the child.

IV. Cabin Crew's Cabin Check After a Decompression

1. Once the aircraft has leveled off and the cockpit crew has stated it is safe to move about, check passengers and the cabin.
2. Reseat passengers away from windblast or danger area if there is an opening in the fuselage.
3. Administer first aid to any injured passengers or crew members.
4. Walk through the cabin and reassure passengers.
5. Check for cabin fires and other potential dangers.
6. Check lavatories for passengers.
7. Have passengers place used oxygen masks in their seat pockets, if possible.

V. Effects of a Decompression

1. Hypoxia

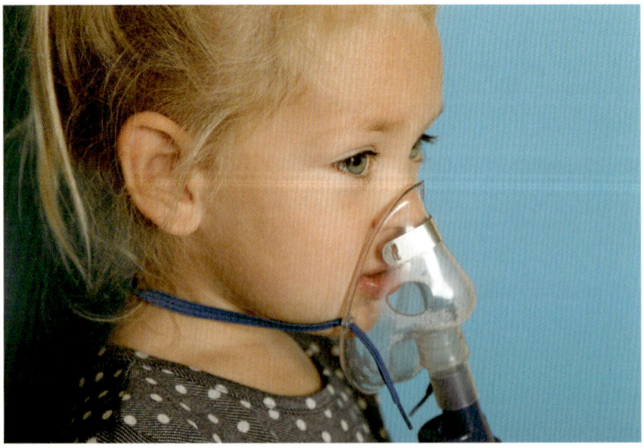

1) Cause

- A lack of oxygen

2) Symptoms

- Increased breathing rate, headache, light-headed or dizzy sensation
- Excessive sleepiness, fatigue, listlessness, tingling or warm sensations
- Impairment of judgment, vision, poor coordination
- Bluish coloration of skin, unconsciousness

3) First Aid

- Administer oxygen immediately.
- Stay with person and reassure them.
- Monitor vital signs.

Vital Signs

There are 4 important signs that indicate the status of the body's vital (life-sustaining) functions. These 4 primary vital signs are: body temperature, respiration, blood pressure, and pulse (heart rate).

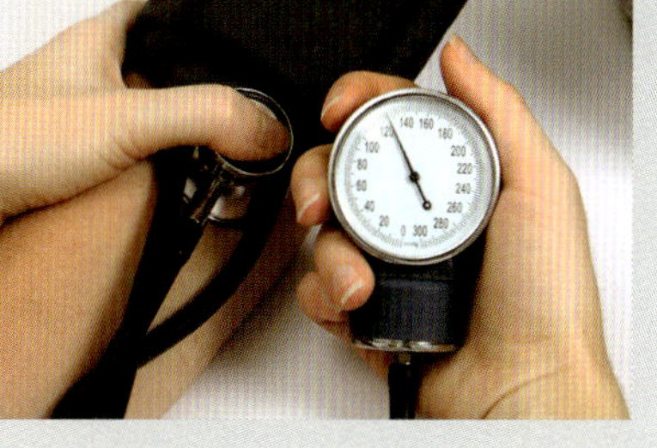

Body temperature: 36.0 - 37.2℃
Respiration: 12 - 20/min, watch, listen and feel
Pulse: 60 - 100/min, Use finger
Blood pressure: 140 - 90mmHg/ 90 - 60mmHg

2. Decompression Sickness

1) Cause

- A side effect caused by trapped or evolved gases due to a sudden loss of pressurization.

2) Symptoms

- Pressure pain in and around joints

- Blockage of pulmonary blood vessels with a corresponding burning pain in the chest
- Tingling, itching, skin rash, visual disturbances, and headaches
- Warm/cold sensations

3) First Aid

- Pain and other symptoms should be relieved after aircraft descent.
- Keep affected area immobile.
- Avoid exercise.

VI. Time of Useful Consciousness: TUC

This is the period of time from the onset of decompression until a person is unable to effectively or adequately perform tasks due to an insufficient supply of oxygen.
The most significant factor that affects TUC is altitude.

Altitude	TUC	
	Rapid Decompression	Unpressurized Aircraft
15,000 ft	15-20 minutes	30 minutes
25,000 ft	2.5 minutes	5 minutes
30,000 ft	30 seconds-1 minute	1-2 minutes
40,000 ft and over	18 seconds	18 seconds

Student Activity - **Team Discussion**

Read the article and answer the questions.

How to survive in an airplane rapid decompression accident

(Source: https://www.travelersunited.org)

Q1. There are two types of decompression. What are they?

Q2. How long can we keep our consciousness at 39,000 ft?

Q3. How can we recognize that a decompression is occurring?

Q4. When decompression occurs, what should passengers, cabin crew, and captain do?

Q5. When the mask doesn't drop, what should the flight attendants or passengers do?

Chapter
12

Emergency Evacuation

When an aircraft accident or incident occurs, an emergency evacuation may be required for the safety of passengers and crew members. Emergency evacuation training is the key to minimize the harmful effects of such events. Failure to evacuate the aircraft in a timely manner may lead to the death or injury of crew and passengers. An in-flight fire, smoke or fume emergency will be dealt with as aggressively as possible by the crew and, if appropriate, an immediate diversion to landing will be initiated. If the emergency is not secured, once on the ground, the most appropriate course of action is to remove the passengers and crew from the risk as a precautionary measure. Likewise, in the event of an uncontrolled engine or airframe fire during ground operations, an aircraft crash during take-off or landing, or any other situation that results in fire or structural failure, the best option available is an immediate evacuation of the aircraft.

I. Initiating Evacuation

An evacuation should be initiated by the PIC; however, in catastrophic events, the PIC may not be able to give this instruction. Cabin crew should be trained to recognize the situations where they are permitted to initiate an evacuation without waiting for an order, and that they may only do so once the aircraft is stationary with engines powered down. Suggested circumstances for cabin crew to initiate evacuations include:

- A fire inside or outside the aircraft that is uncontained and getting worse
- Dense smoke in the cabin that is threatening life
- Obvious destruction of the aircraft

STR/AFP via Getty Images

When making the decision to initiate an evacuation, cabin crew must evaluate the level of danger and the consequences that a delay in decision-making may lead to. Smoke or fire that is out of control would definitely require a rapid decision because of the danger presented to the occupants of the aircraft. If cabin crew consider that an evacuation may be required, they must attempt to contact the flight crew in order to inform them of the situation and await instructions. If contact with the flight crew is not possible, cabin crew should initiate the evacuation. Any evacuation requires crew coordination because not all crew members may be aware that a life-threatening situation exists. There are several possible methods of communication, depending on their availability:

- Public address
- Interphone
- Megaphone
- Evacuation alarm (if applicable)
- Initiation of commands

II. Types of Emergency Evacuation

The emergency evacuation is divided into unplanned and planned, depending on whether there is time to prepare for the impact or not.

1. Unplanned Emergency Evacuation

Many evacuations are not planned and occur with no prior warning on stand, during taxi, take-off or landing. In an unplanned emergency landing, there is no time for preparation. So to prepare for the unplanned emergency situation, cabin crew perform the regular safety work and check, which are to sit on the ready position, conduct 30 second review. The 30 second review carried out by cabin crew during take-off and landing helps to keep them mentally prepared to act with little or no notice during critical stages of flight. And cabin crew have passengers sit and fasten their seat belts, secure the cabin and galleys during take-off and landing to prepare the unexpected emergency situation. Passenger safety briefing and exit briefing are also one of the regular safety works of cabin crew. If cabin crew are well trained to respond to any situation, possibility of survival in unplanned emergency goes up.

2. Planned Emergency Evacuation

In-flight emergencies may result in the diversion of the aircraft and a planned emergency evacuation. Cabin crew will have some time to prepare the cabin and passengers for evacuation after landing.

III. Planned Emergency Evacuation Procedure

Emergency evacuation procedures are established on three criteria which are **Survive the impact**, **Escape the aircraft**, and **Survive the environment**.

1. Cabin Preparation: To Survive the Impact

1) Briefing of Cabin Crew

If the captain recognizes the emergency situation and judges that an emergency landing/ditching is necessary, he or she should first communicate and coordinate with the duty purser and then the duty purser will share the information with other crew members.

- Type of emergency (including emergency landing or ditching, aircraft problem, weather conditions)
- Time for preparation
- Signal to brace and who will give it
- Signal to evacuate and who will give it
- Special instructions

2) Briefing of Passengers

The captain or duty purser will advise the passengers of an emergency situation, depending on the time available and procedures. The initial announcement will typically include:

- Explanation of the nature of the emergency
- Necessity to prepare the cabin
- Requirement to follow the instructions of the cabin crew

Duty Purser Announcement

Ladies and gentlemen, we need your attention. We will have to make an emergency landing/ditching in about _____minutes. We are trained to handle this situation. Remain calm and follow the instructions of our cabin crew.
Cross check!

At the appropriate time according to operator procedures, the cabin crew will perform an emergency safety demonstration/briefing giving the passengers additional information relating to the planned emergency evacuation. The aim of the briefing is to give passengers as much information as possible. The amount of time available will determine the extent of the briefing. When reading the briefing, the duty purser should pause at key points in order to allow the cabin crew time to demonstrate and check passenger compliance.

(1) Pick up Catering Items & Secure Seatbacks/Tray Table

Pick up and stow all catering items (meal trays, cups, and glasses). Return seatbacks. Stow tray tables, in-seat video units and footrests.

Duty Purser Announcement

When the cabin crew come to your row, pass your food tray and all other service items to the aisle for pick up. At this time, bring seatbacks to the upright position and stow all tray tables. Stow footrest and in-seat video units.
Cross check!

(2) Remove Sharp Objects, Loosen Tight Clothing & Stow Carry-On Items

Remove all shoes for ditching and stow them under the seat or in the overhead bins. Ensure all carry-on items are stowed in approved stowage locations.

Duty Purser Announcement

Remove all sharp objects such as pens and jewelry. Also remove loose objects such as neckties and scarves. Remove spike heeled shoes. (Remove all shoes. Put them underneath a seat or in the overhead bins.) Put all of these items in carry-on baggage. Remove eyeglasses before landing and put them in your sock or a side coat pocket. Do not put anything in the seat pocket in front of you. Put all carry-on items under the seat or in the overhead bin. Cabin crew will be in the aisles to assist you. Cross check!

(3) Don Life Vests (Only Ditching)

Use cabin crew life vests to demonstrate proper life vest donning procedures for adults. Provide life vests for infants/small children and individually brief passengers traveling with infants/small children.

> **Duty Purser Announcement**
>
> Locate the life vest under or on the side of your seat and remove it. Remove the life vest from the pouch by pulling on the tab. To put the life vest on, slip it over your head. Adjust the straps around your waist. Do not inflate the vest inside the aircraft. As you leave the aircraft, pull down the red tabs to inflate the vest. The vest can also be inflated by blowing into the tube(s). For those traveling with infants or small children, the cabin crew will assist you in putting vests on the children. For anyone else needing help, cabin crew will assist you. Cross check!

(4) Fasten Seat Belts

Demonstrate seat belt operation. Ensure all passengers' seat belts are secured low and tight.

> **Duty Purser Announcement**
>
> Fasten your seat belt. Place the metal tip into the buckle and tighten the strap low and secure about you. When told to release your seat belt, lift the top of the buckle. Cross check!

(5) Demonstrate Bracing Positions

Explain the bracing positions as applicable. Inform passengers of the signal to brace one minute (altitude 1,000 feet) prior to impact. ('Fasten Seat Belt' Sign 4 times simultaneously and PA 'Brace for Impact' twice, cabin crew yell the command "Brace!") Tell passengers to remain in bracing position until the aircraft comes to a complete stop.

Duty Purser Announcement

The signal to brace will be given just before landing. The signal will be 'Brace for Impact', and cabin crew will command you to brace. When instructed to brace for impact, place your feet on the floor, cross your arms and put hands on the seat in front of you. Put your head on your arms. If you cannot reach the seatback in front of you, or if there is no seat in front of you, lean forward as far as you can and wrap your arms tightly under your legs or grab your ankles and put your head on your knees. Hold your bracing position until the aircraft comes to a complete stop. Then follow the instructions of your crew. Cross check!

Bulkhead	Non-Bulkhead

(6) Review Exit Locations

Point out exits and emergency lighting as in a demonstration. Remind passengers not everyone will exit the boarding door and the closest exit may be behind them.

Duty Purser Announcement

Exits on this aircraft are 4 doors, 2 doors forward and 2 doors rear, 4 overwing window exits over the wings. The cabin crew are pointing to the exits nearest to you, and be aware your closest exit may be behind you. Emergency track lighting installed near the floor will lead you to an exit, which is identified by a red light. When instructed to evacuate, go to the nearest exit. When you reach the ground, run away from the aircraft. Cross check!

(7) Show Passenger Safety Information Card and Encourage Passengers to Review

Duty Purser Announcement

Take the Safety Information Card from the seat pocket in front of you and review seat belt operation, bracing position, life vest operation, exit locations, and exit operation. Cabin crew will be in the aisles to assist you and answer any questions. Thank you for your attention.
Cross check!

3) Preparing the Cabin, Galleys and Lavatories

During normal procedures for take-off and landing, the cabin secure procedures are carried out to prepare the cabin for an unplanned emergency. During a planned emergency, as it is known that an evacuation is highly likely, some additional cabin preparations can be carried out to further mitigate risks, depending on the circumstances and time available:

(1) Check/Secure Cabin, Galleys and Lavatories

Check that carry-on baggage is properly stowed and seat belts are low and secure, seatbacks are upright, and that tray tables, in-seat video units, and footrest are stowed. Stow carts and carry-on boxes.

(2) Additional Cabin Preparations

IFE, Internet and telecommunications systems, where fitted, should be switched off. Also, galley power and water supply should be turned off.

4) Select/Brief Assistants

Procedures should include enlisting the help of able-bodied passengers (ABPs) who will be useful during the evacuation. The selection of ABPs may be based on their physical strength and capabilities as well as their ability to understand instructions and respond appropriately. Deadheading crew, off-duty company crew members, military, police and fire service personnel are good choices because they are accustomed to following instructions and have the required strength and dexterity.

Briefing several ABPs at each door will help ensure sufficient help is available and briefing them collectively rather than assigning individual roles will ensure the greatest chance of procedures being understood and carried out. Other ABPs can be briefed to assist special categories of passengers who may require additional help. The cabin crew should ensure that ABPs are assigned to passengers that require assistance to evacuate the aircraft. These passengers include:

- Passengers with reduced mobility
- Elderly
- Unaccompanied minors
- People traveling alone with more than one child

These passengers will need assistance from ABPs during the evacuation. When time permits, reseat an ABP with each passenger requiring assistance.

5) Make Final Preparations

(1) Recheck Cabin/Galleys

Make the cabin lights darker than outside.

(2) Notify Captain

Notify captain when cabin and galley are secure and passengers are briefed and prepared.

(3) Review Evacuation Duties

Refer to the **cabin crew duty assignment chart** of each aircraft type in this manual.

(4) Sit on Jumpseat

Sit on your assigned jumpseat with lap belt pulled secure and as low as possible. Adjust shoulder harness to hold back firmly against the seatback.

(5) Turn on Emergency Lights

Duty purser turn on the emergency lights before sitting on the jumpseat.

2. Bracing for Impact: To Survive the Impact

Upon the signal from the captain – 'Fasten Seat Belt' sign 4 times simultaneously and PA 'Brace for Impact' twice, assume a full bracing position immediately and command passengers to brace 3 times. "충격방지 자세!, Brace" (*3)

Remain in bracing position until the aircraft stops forward movement.

Forward Facing Jumpseat	Aft Facing Jumpseat

There are two types of jumpseats: forward facing and aft facing. When a moving plane stops suddenly, our body, head, arms and legs will be thrust forward suddenly because of momentum. To minimize injury, cabin crew sitting in the forward jumpseat should pull his or her chin toward the chest to protect the head, hold the legs firmly together and planted to the floor, with the palms tucked firmly beneath the thighs.

Cabin crew sitting in the aft facing jumpseat should press the head firmly against the back of the jumpseat, hold the legs firmly together and planted to the floor, with the palms tucked firmly beneath the thighs.

3. Escape the Aircraft

You survive the impact, thanks to the brace position. Next is the emergency evacuation which should be initiated by the captain. Cabin crew should wait for the captain's instruction.

PIC's PA	Evaluation	Cabin Crew Duty
After Landing PA: "This is the captain." "Remain seated, remain seated." **Rejected take-off PA:** "This is the captain." "Remain seated, remain seated."	Emergency Evacuation Not Required	Stay at right position for the next steps.
"Attention, crew at station."	Emergency Evacuation Anticipated	Be prepared for emergency evacuation at right position.
"This is the captain. Evacuate, evacuate!"	Emergency Evacuation Required	Command the emergency evacuation.

1) Verify If Evacuation is Required

Cabin crew should evaluate the situation to decide evacuation when the aircraft stops moving. First of all, captain's PA is important to evaluate the situation. If there's no PA or other actions taken, cabin crew should contact captain by using emergency signal. But if there is no response from the cockpit in spite of an attempt to contact, evacuate passengers under the following conditions when aircraft stops moving.

- Severe structural damage
- Threatening fire or smoke
- Passengers are in imminent danger

2) Initiating Evacuation

When the captain announces "This is the captain. **Evacuate! Evacuate!**" or gives the evacuation signal, all cabin crew should commence their evacuation duties.

- Give motivational commands.

> 벨트 풀어! 나와! 짐 버려!
> Release seat belt! Get out! Leave everything!
>
> 벨트 풀어! 구명복 입어! 나와! 짐 버려!*
> Release seat belt! Get your life vest! Get out! Leave everything!
>
> * In case of emergency ditching

- Maintain motivational commands and direct the evacuation.

• Release seat belt, grab flashlight (if necessary) and proceed to nearest or designated exit.

• Command assistants, as necessary, to assess conditions and activate exits.

3) Assess Condition for Evacuation

• Look for structural damage, fire, or if exit is underwater or obstructed.

• Assess type of emergency (landing/water).

Situations		Most Desirable Exits
Fire		Opposite the fire
Belly Landing	 imageBROKER/ Alany Stack Photo	All
Main Gear Collapse	 FLHC 8/Alamy Stock Photo	Low doors / Overwing window exit
Nose Gear Collapse		Forward door / Forward windows
Water	 CC BY 2.0 by ©zvoorwaarden bekijken	Doors above the surface of the water

4) Activate Exit and Evacuation

- Quickly confirm armed status of exit.
- Open exit. Utilize all available exits by requesting passenger assistance if responsible for more than one exit.
- If exit is jammed or slide/raft is not usable, attempt to open it again and (if necessary), redirect passengers to an alternate exit using appropriate commands.

Bad Exit Command

: 탈출구 불량! 건너편으로! 저쪽으로! Bad exit! Cross over! Go that way!

- Once the door and associated escape device is ready and confirmed operational, the cabin crew should instruct passengers in the cabin to move towards it and prepare to evacuate.

Good Exit Command

: 이쪽으로! Come this way!

Command Passengers to Evacuate

: 뛰어 내려가! 멀리 피해! Jump and slide! Move away!

: 구명복 부풀려! 안쪽으로! Inflate your life vest! Step into the raft!*

* In case of emergency ditching

5) Continually Assess Conditions

- If exit becomes unusable, block exit verbally using **bad exit command** and redirect passengers to an alternate exit, giving appropriate commands.
- If many passengers are waiting in line at any exit, consider redirecting to less crowded exits.
- If passengers are piling up at bottom of slide, temporarily halt evacuation.

6) Evacuate the Aircraft

- After all remaining passengers have been evacuated, or if it is not possible to remain in the cabin, cabin crew should evacuate through the first available exit after taking the applicable emergency equipment from the aircraft (e.g., megaphone, first aid kit, flashlight).

- When evacuating during a ditching, cabin crew should evacuate through their own assigned exit, where possible, so that they can assume control of the slide/raft.

4. Post-Evacuation: For Surviving the Environment

Once outside the aircraft, the cabin crew is responsible for the passengers until relieved by the authorities or emergency services. Until this help arrives, the cabin crew should:

- Direct passengers upwind and away from the aircraft.
- Assemble passengers and direct passengers away from fuel, fire, and vehicles.
- Assist passengers and provide first aid.
- Start survival planning (if in a remote location).

Student Activity - **Team Discussion**

Scan the QR code to read the article and answer the questions.

Did Asiana passengers ignore safety messages?

(Source : https://edition.cnn.com)

Q1. According to the article, what safety procedures did passengers ignore during evacuation?

Q2. Some passengers argue that it is basic instinct to grab their carry-on luggage before evacuating the aircraft. What do you think? What would you do if you have your passport and valuables in your carry-on luggage in the overhead bin during evacuation?

Q3. Imagine that you are one of the cabin crew on the R2 door and you experience a sudden stop before take-off. You see a fire in the R3 door area, hear people screaming and could smell burning. What emergency procedures should you take?

Student Activity - Part III Practical Evaluation

Situational Emergency Procedures				
Subject	Contents	1	2	3
Evacuation Procedures & Commands	Seat belt & Shoulder Harness / Ready Position			
	Brace Position (Forward/Aft)			
	Communicate with Cockpit			
	Motivational Commands (Landing/Ditching)			
	Evacuation Horn Shut-off/ Flashlight Pickup			
	Assess Outside Condition			
	Confirm Door Mode			
	Hold Assist Handle & Open Exit			
	Pull Manual Inflation Handle			
	Hold Assist Handle & Get Dedicated Assist Space			
	Block Passenger			
	Verify Slide Inflation			
	Evacuation Commands (Landing/Ditching)			

Decompression & Firefighting				
Subject	Contents	1	2	3
Response	Take immediate response to decompression			
Procedures	Follow the procedures to fight the 'oven' fire			
	Follow the procedures to fight the 'lavatory' fire			

PART 4

Aviation Security

Aviation security is a combination of human and material resources to safeguard civil aviation against unlawful interference. Unlawful interference could be acts of terrorism, sabotage, threat to life and property, communication of false threat, bombing, etc. (ICAO Annex 17). Aircraft security includes all performances to prevent aircraft hijacking, bomb threat, and any other illegal attempts which hinder an aircraft's operations. Airlines have the responsibilities of aircraft security and they must implement step-by-step security procedures to protect aircraft from sabotage.

Chapter

13

Aircraft Security Procedures

I. Check-In

Airline ground staff should identify passengers with passports or ID cards, and also make sure whether passengers carry dangerous goods or not. For the safety and security reason, **SRI (Security Removed Items)** such as golf clubs and weaponry like knives are subject to be removed by personnel. Those items collected at the X-Ray check must be carried in the cargo area (loaded in bulk) and be returned at the baggage claim area.

Examples of SRI

• Hand Cuffs

• Knives

• Pocket Knife

• Scissors

• Manicure Sets

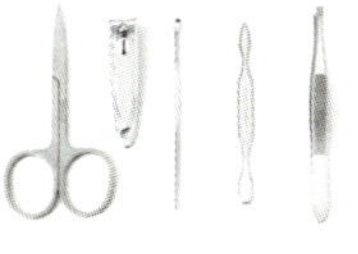

• Weapons

• Aerosols

• Sparkles

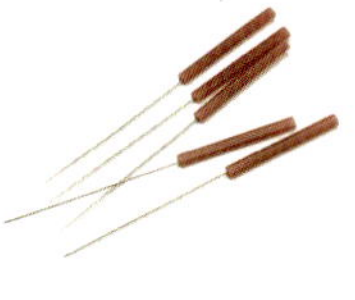

• Golf Sets

• Baseball Bats

• Hockey Sticks

II. Before Departure

1. Restricted Areas

Only authorized personnel and passengers, as well as screened baggage, mail and cargo should have access to the aircraft, airside and/or other restricted areas. Cabin crew should report to the applicable authorities of any situation that could affect the security of a flight, and challenge anyone attempting to gain access to the aircraft without authorization or proper identification. Potential security breaches should be reported to the PIC and the relevant security department of the organization.

Sorbis / Shutterstock.com

2. Aircraft Security Check

Before flight, under duty purser's instruction, cabin crew shall perform security check according to aviation security regulation. However, the security regulation of destination country shall be observed in case it is different from that of the airline. The check should include all compartments that are accessible and are in general use by cabin crew and passengers on a flight. This should be completed before passengers embark and after passengers disembark. If suspicious items are found, cabin crew shall report to the captain or duty purser immediately without touching them, so that they can be reported to the related authority.

Sefa Karacan/Anadolu Agency via Getty Images

Pre-flight Security Checklist

Area		Check Items	S	U	N/A
Cabin	Magazine Rack	Inside of magazine racks			
	Seat	Inside of seat pockets: Alert1 & EU only			
		Under the seat cushions and life vests: Alert1 & UK only			
		Upside of seats			
		Both sidewalls including windows			
		Compartments around seats			
		Sidewall stowage bins			
	Aisle	Inside of all overhead bins			
		Corners near the bulkhead and curtain			
		Floor			
	Jumpseat	Crew jumpseats and life vests			
		Emergency equipment storage			
	Door	Corners near the door			
		Inside of coatrooms			
	CRA	Crew rest area			
	VCC	Video control center			
Lavatory	Facility	Area around the lavatory door, wall and ceiling			
		Area around the toilet			
	Compartment	Towel containers and tissue dispensers			
		Area under sink			
		Rubbish bins			
		Compartments in the back of mirror			
Galley	Compartment	All storage compartments (Ovens, refrigerators, bars)			
		Ceiling, wall and floor			
		Rubbish bins and towel containers			
		Compartments in the ceiling			
		Inside of cart lift (Elevator)			
	Cart	Carts sealing			

LAVATORY
Area around the lavatory door, wall and ceiling
• Inspect the space behind the lavatory door when it is opened. • Inspect for any signs of tampering on the lavatory wall and ceiling.
Area around the toilet
• Inspect the area behind the toilet. • Open the toilet lid and inspect inside.
Towel containers and tissue dispensers
• Open and inspect all compartments for stowing toilet papers and tissues. • Inspect the area above carefully since it is easy for suspicious items to be hidden under/behind them.
Area under sink
• Open and inspect the compartment under sink. • Inspect with care since there is pipe in the compartment.
Rubbish bins
• Take out the rubbish bins and inspect inside.
Compartments in the back of mirror
• Open the mirrors (if able to open) of lavatories and inspect the compartments inside.
GALLEY
All storage compartments (ovens, refrigerators, bars)
• Open and inspect the oven, refrigerator and all compartments.
Ceiling, walls and floor
• Check walls, ceiling and floor. Inspect for any signs of tampering.
Rubbish bins and towel containers
• Take out rubbish bins and towel containers then inspect inside.
Compartments in the ceiling
• Pull down ceiling compartments and inspect inside.
Inside of cart lift (Elevator) [A380, B747]
• Open the cart lift and inspect inside. • Inspect empty space when the cart lift is lifted.
Cart sealing
• [Alert 3,2] Randomly check 20% of seal numbers of catering items loaded on the aircraft, comparing with the seal number list provided by caterer. • [Alert 1] Check 100% of seal numbers of catering items loaded on the aircraft, comparing with seal number list provided by caterer.
CABIN
Inside of seat pockets (100% Check for Alert Level 1 only. However, 100% Check for flights departing from EU)
• Inspect the inside of seat pocket after taking out service items (hand + visual search).
Under the seat cushions and life vests (100% Check for Alert Level 1 only. However, 5% Check for FLT departing EU except LHR – 10% for flights departing LHR)

- Remove seat cushions and inspect the seats.
- Inspect life vests and the stowage by hands.
- If sealed, check if the seal is tampered, and if tampered, inspect the life vest and the stowage by hands.

Upside of seats

- Inspect if there are any suspicious items on the seats.
- Remove service items (blankets, pillows etc.) from the seats and inspect for suspicious items.

Behind headrest

- Inspect space behind headrest (some FR/PR seats).

Both sidewalls including windows

- Inspect the obscure space between window seats and the sidewall.

Inside of all overhead bin

- Open and inspect the overhead bins.

Corners near the bulkhead and curtain

- Open curtains and inspect walls and corners.

Floor

- Inspect for any suspicious items on the floor.
- Inspect for any signs of tampering of the floor carpet.

Crew jumpseat and life vest

- Unfold jumpseats and inspect inside.
- Open and inspect the stowage of emergency equipment (life vests, etc.) under jumpseats.

Emergency equipment storage

- Open and inspect the storage of emergency equipment.

Corners near the door

- Inspect corners and the bottom of doors.
- Open and inspect the curtains around doors.

Inside of coatrooms

- Open and inspect coatrooms for any suspicious items besides bassinets or emergency equipment (EMK, etc.).

Inside of magazine racks

- Inspect inside of magazine racks and check for any suspicious items besides magazines.

Crew rest area

- Open and inspect all compartments. (If sealed, see if seals are tampered.)
- Open the bunk curtains completely and inspect mattress area, storage pocket, etc.
- If there are seats in the crew rest area, inspect the seats and the bottom of seat cushions.

Video control center

- Open and inspect all compartments in and around video control center.
- Inspect spaces between the video players.

3. Boarding Pass Check

During passengers' boarding, cabin crew shall check boarding passes to prevent unauthorized aircraft access. Cabin crew should request identification of each un-ticketed, unidentified person on or in the vicinity of the aircraft or any secure area. If the person refuses or cannot produce proper identification, try to keep the person under surveillance and notify ground staff or law enforcement.

III. In-flight

1. Cabin/Lavatory Check

During the flight, cabin crew should be alert to any suspicious/unusual passenger activities, security matters, hazardous materials and unidentified articles. If any suspicious activity or items are found, report to the captain through interphone directly. When it's not possible to use interphone in case of emergency cases such as cockpit entry violation, security breach in the cabin or hijacking, cabin crew shall notify the cockpit using hijacking warning bell.

2. Handling Clear Zone

Clear zone is the area of cabin immediately in front of the cockpit door, including galleys and lavatories. Passenger presence without any reasons, such as use of lavatory, should be discouraged by captain and cabin crew. If an unlawful interference, such as in-flight disturbance, is expected or occurs, **clear zone declare** should be activated and the cockpit door should be fully locked. If the passenger threat appears to advance to life-threatening behavior, attempt of cockpit intrusion and actual intrusion, the captain directs designated cabin crew to declare clear zone. And cabin crew should take the following actions:

- Passengers should be in their seats and a cart should be placed in front of cockpit door.(Captain turns on the seat belt sign.)
- Passengers' assistance and cooperation should be requested in efforts such as blocking the clear zone, etc.

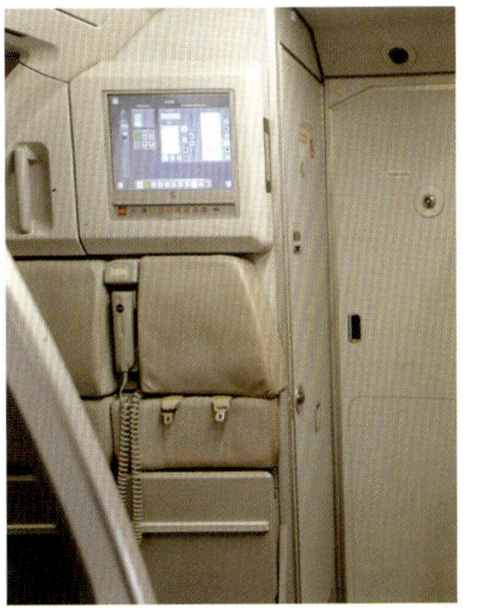

3. Reinforced Flight Deck Door

After 9/11, airlines installed doors featuring sturdier locking mechanism controlled by switches inside the cockpit. The principal intent of a reinforced flight deck door is to ensure the security of the flight deck by restricting access. Operators should provide the crew with appropriate guidance, procedures and instructions for use when a reinforced flight deck door is fitted.

SETH MCALLISTER/AFP via Getty Images

ERIC CABANIS/AFP via Getty Images

IV. After Flight

Cabin crew shall check to see if there are any items left behind and remaining passengers after each flight operation and also prevent unauthorized/unidentified persons and articles from having access to aircraft.

Student Activity - **Team Discussion**

Read the article and answer the questions.

Six Ryanair passengers miss flights as they board wrong plane

(Source: https://www.irishexaminer.com)

Q1. Summarize the article. What is it about?

Q2. What are the main reasons of the security incident?

Q3. Why is this kind of security incident a big issue in the airline industry? And how can it be prevented from happening?

Chapter

14

Handling Unruly Passengers

Safety and security are considered the airline industry's top priorities. However, disruptive passengers have become more prevalent over the past several years and unruly passenger incidents have become a very real and serious threat to both safety and security.

International Civil Aviation Organization (ICAO) defined a disruptive passenger as "a passenger who fails to respect the rules of conduct at an airport or on board an aircraft or to follow the instructions of the airport staff or crew members and thereby disturbs the good order and discipline at an airport or on board the aircraft."

ICAO has also defined a four tier threat level hierarchy. Although all National Aviation Authorities (NAA) do not follow these specific definitions, they provide valuable guidance to operators in determining the seriousness of an unruly passenger incident and in developing their policies on appropriate level of response. The ICAO level of threat specifics are as follows:

I. Level 1

1. Types of Unlawful Acts

- Interference caused by suspicious behavior or **verbal threat**
- Sexual harassment, smoking

- Use of non-approved electronic devices
- Making noise, such as abusive language
- **Not following the legitimate official instructions** given by the captain, etc.
- Occupying the airplane and staging a sit-down demonstration on the airplane without disembarking from the airplane after the airplane lands

Level 1 Case 1

Abusive flyer offloaded from aircraft

An aircraft returned to its parking bay after taxiing for take-off to offload a passenger who had become abusive with a cabin crew member. 'The cabin crew member asked him to put his seat upright, but received verbal abuse in response', said an airline official. It is not known whether the passenger was drunk. When informed of the incident, the captain decided to turn the aircraft back to the parking bay to offload the unruly passenger.

(Source: Gerighty(©2010). English for Cabin Crew 1st edition. Heinle, Cengage Learning)

2. Crew Action

- **Verbal warning or issuing a warning card** for resolving the situation
- Report to the captain and share the information among cabin crew.
- Surveillance on other passengers
- If necessary, declare a clear zone.

Warning Card

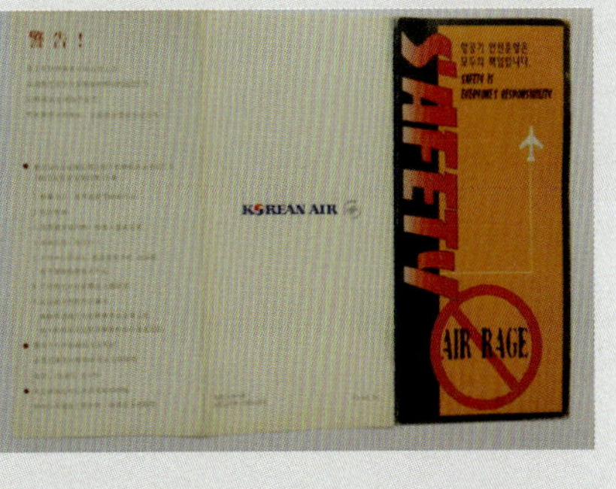

Unruly or disruptive passengers should be made aware of the consequences of their actions and the type of measures that will be taken to stop the disruptive behavior. Those conditions can be conveyed verbally or in writing and should include as a minimum: restricting the unruly passenger's alcohol consumption; prohibiting the unruly passenger from behaving in a manner that might cause concern to other passengers and crew members; and the passenger's mandatory compliance with all directions given to him or her by any member of the crew. An example used by some air carriers is the notification warning cards presented by crew members to unruly/disruptive passengers in flight. The cards call for the person to desist or suffer the consequences of having the incident referred to the police and face the possibility of a fine, arrest, prosecution, or imprisonment.

II. Level 2

1. Types of Unlawful Acts (Physically Violent Behavior)

- If **Level 1** behavior becomes worse
- Physical attack
- Malicious operations of the entrance, emergency exit, devices that hinder the security and flight of the aircraft
- Obstructing the duties of the crew, doing harm to other persons after drinking alcohol or taking drugs, threatening, or engaging in deception which hinders the security of the flight

Level 2 Case 1

Woman who hit attendants jailed after forced landing of Tokyo flight

A 42-year-old woman has been jailed after causing a trans-Pacific flight to be diverted to Anchorage, Alaska. The woman was aboard the Delta Airlines flight from Tokyo to New York when, about 45 minutes into the flight, she began assaulting a flight attendant who was offering a beverage service. Flight attendants tried to calm her, but she continued screaming profanities in Japanese and hit four flight attendants before being handcuffed and seat-belted in her seat. She continued to struggle and unbuckled her seat belt several times, causing flight attendants to set up 30-minutes rotation to watch her. Pilots were forced to dump 70,000 pounds of jet fuel to land in Anchorage and hand her over to local police.

(Source: Gerighty(©2010). English for Cabin Crew 1st edition. Heinle, Cengage Learning)

Level 2 Case 2

One too many

A passenger was arrested on Friday after his flight landed on charges that he assaulted and intimidated the flight crew. The man drank five glasses of wine after boarding the flight in Atlanta, Georgia, authorities said. He became abusive when flight attendants refused to serve him a sixth drink. When the senior flight attendant arrived to try to calm him, he grabbed her arms and hands. Flight attendants armed themselves with fire extinguisher and positioned drinks trolleys in the aisles in case the man tried to get into the cockpit.

(Source: Gerighty(©2010). English for Cabin Crew 1st edition. Heinle, Cengage Learning)

Level 2 Case 3

Vegas flight lands in Denver after air rage incident

A US Airline en-route to Las Vegas was diverted to Denver after a passenger tried to open an exterior door on the plane, officials say. The man had reportedly consumed alcohol before and during the flight. 'There was a disturbance on board involving an unruly passenger, and the pilots decided to divert to Denver,' local police said in a statement.

(Source: Gerighty(©2010). English for Cabin Crew 1st edition. Heinle, Cengage Learning)

Level 2 Case 4

Drunk passenger jailed after going on rampage at 30,000ft

A drunken airline passenger went on a rampage at 30,000 feet after cabin crew caught him trying to get into the first-class section. During the nine-and-a-half hour flight, the man, who was traveling in economy class, walked up and down the aisles shouting abuse, reducing passengers to tears and causing his own daughter, aged 15, to go and sit with crew to hide from him. He was jailed for eight months after pleading guilty to being drunk on an aircraft.

(Source: Gerighty(©2010). English for Cabin Crew 1st edition. Heinle, Cengage Learning)

2. Crew Action

- **Restrain and detain disruptive passenger promptly by using security equipment.**
- Declare clear zone.
- Report to the captain and share the information among cabin crew.
- Surveillance on other passengers

Restraining Devices

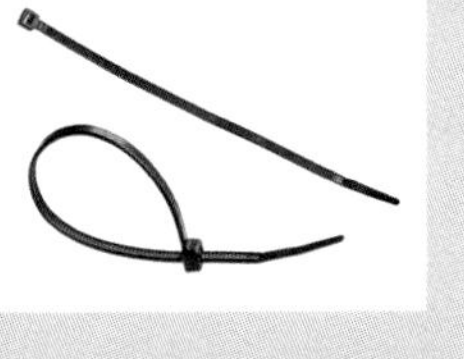

Crew need to be aware that a situation can escalate at any moment and sometimes without warning. In turn, crew members must attempt to defuse a critical situation until it becomes clear that there is no way to resolve it verbally. Some carriers have devices to restrain a physically confrontational passenger. Applying restraining devices should be used when all conciliatory approaches have been exhausted. Once restraints have been used, they should remain on the passenger for the duration of the flight even if he/she promises good behavior.

Notify Miranda Rights

Right after restraining an unruly passenger, notify Miranda rights to the passenger.

체포 시 고지사항(Notice upon arrest) (형사 소송법 제 72조)
귀하를 (승객 및 승무원 폭행)의 현행범으로 체포합니다.
귀하는 변호인을 선임할 수 있으며 변명할 권리가 있습니다.
(변명의 기회부여) 하고 싶은 말이 있습니까?
(외국인의 경우) 도착 후 당신이 체포된 사실을 귀국의 영사관원에게 통보해 줄 수 있으며, 그들과 접촉하여 교통할 수 있습니다.

You are under arrest in the act of committing (   ).
You have the right to retain an attorney and defend yourself.
Do you wish to say anything in answer to the charge?
(For foreigners) At arrival, your arrest will be notified to the consulate of your country and you may be able to contact and communicate with their staff.

III. Level 3

1. Types of Unlawful Acts (Life Threatening Behavior)

- If **Level 2** behavior becomes worse
- Life threat by displaying or use of weapon etc.

Level 3 Case

Airplane violence: unruly Delta passenger trying to open exit door hit with wine bottle

(Source: https://youtu.be/VStx0Ro7SY4)

2. Crew Action

- Restrain and detain perpetrator promptly by using security equipment.
- Declare clear zone.
- Report to the captain and share the information among cabin crew.
- Surveillance on other passengers
- If necessary, implement procedure to handle explosive devices or biochemical substances in the aircraft.

IV. Level 4

1. Types of Unlawful Acts (Attempted or actual breach of the flight deck)

- If **level 3** behavior becomes worse
- Hijacking or attempt to hijack an aircraft
- Sabotage or causing damage to aircraft, taking a person hostage

Level 4 Case

Bangladesh plane hijacker shot dead by special forces

(Source: https://edition.cnn.com)

2. Crew Action

- Restrain and detain perpetrator promptly by using security equipment.
- Declare clear zone.
- Report to the captain and share the information among cabin crew.
- Surveillance on other passengers
- If necessary, implement procedure to handle explosive devices or biochemical substances in the aircraft.

Student Activity - Team Discussion

Read the article and answer the questions.

Unruly passenger caused by alcohol consumption

(Source: https://www.dailymail.co.uk)

Q1. In this case, what is the level of unlawful act?

Q2. If you are a cabin crew, how do you react in this situation?

Q3. What kinds of restraining devices are loaded on aircraft?

Q4. Notify Miranda rights to the passenger.

Chapter

15

Bomb Threat, Finding a Bomb Onboard, and Hijacking

I. Bomb Threat

1.On the Ground

- Deplane all persons from the aircraft by captain's direction and comply with the authority personnel if they request cooperation.
- Cabin crew may conduct security check regarding **pre-flight security checklist**, in accordance with the PIC order.
- Report the cabin check result to the PIC and take action accordingly.
- Monitor closely a person who has suspicious behavior during or after boarding.

2. In-flight

- Each crew member must monitor closely if there is any passenger who behaves suspiciously and strengthen the access control to cockpit door.
- Conduct security check according to **pre-flight security checklist**.
- Report the cabin check result to the PIC and take action accordingly.
- After safe landing, take action immediately to deplane all the passengers in a swift and orderly manner with carry-on items.

• All the crew members should deplane and move to a safe place after deplaning all the passengers.

Bomb Threat Case

Flight makes an emergency landing after threatening message written on toilet

(Source: https://www.news.com.au)

II. Finding Bomb Onboard

1. On the Ground

• Report immediately to the PIC by interphone.

• The following information should be included (shape, size, type, quantity, location and so on).

• Also report it to ground staff so that they can deliver it to the appropriate authorities.

• The duty purser shall keep the bomb out of reach and deplane all passengers as quickly as possible with their personal belongings.

• All crew members also should quickly move to a safe place.

Chung Sung Jun/Getty Images

2. In-flight

• Report immediately to the PIC by interphone as soon as a bomb is found in the cabin and report it to all cabin crews.

• When reporting to PIC, include the shape, size, type, quantity, location and other information about the bomb.

- Prevent unauthorized handling of the device until the decision to move the explosive to the least risky bomb location is made.
- Handle the suspected device in accordance to the procedure of LRBL (Least Risk Bomb Location).
- Continue to search the aircraft to ensure no other devices are on board.
- Let passengers deplane immediately after landing.
- All crew members should quickly move to safe area after deplaning all the passengers from the aircraft.

Least-Risk Bomb Locations

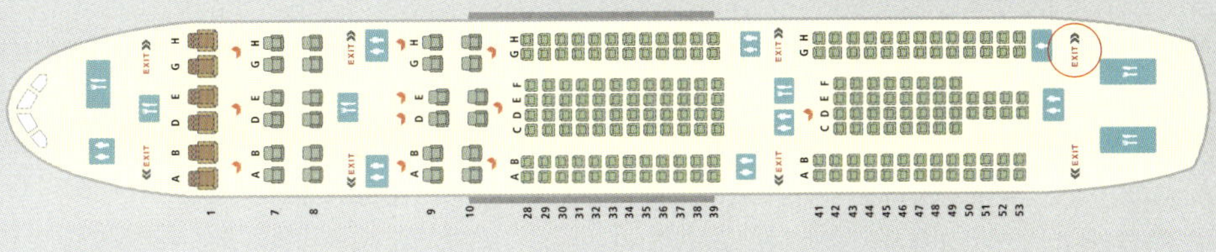

'Least Risk Bomb Location' is the R side rear door of each airplane.

Actions to be Taken to Move the Explosive to the LRBL

1. Disarm the door.
2. Place hard luggage at bottom of door, stacking to the center of the door.
3. Soak a blanket or soft clothing in non-flammable liquids.
4. Place the wet blanket/clothing on top of luggage. And then place explosive-proof mat on the wet blanket/clothing.
5. Two persons move the bomb cautiously onto the center of the mat, above or below the porthole.
6. Fold up half of the mat, with the opened part facing the porthole.
7. Place 25cm of wet material on top and all around the bomb.
8. Pile available carry-on baggage, clothing or seat cushions to fill remaining space up to the ceiling and out to the aisle.
9. Tie nylons, men's ties, headsets, etc. to stabilize the prepared LRBL.

III. Hijacking

Aircraft hijacking is the unlawful seizure of an aircraft by an individual or a group. In most cases, the pilot is forced to fly according to the orders of the hijackers. Occasionally, however, the hijackers have flown the aircraft themselves, such as the September 11 attacks.

Aircraft Hijacking Cases

Indian Airlines flight IC814 was hijacked on 24 December, 1999. The flight was on its way back to Delhi, India from Kathmandu, Nepal with 176 passengers and crew on board. The hijackers demanded the release of Pakistani terrorist Maulana Masood Azhar (the secretary of the terror group) along with 35 other militants who were captured and incarcerated in Indian prisons.

1. Cabin Crew Procedure

The safety of the passengers and crew is the first consideration when an aircraft is hijacked. When a hijacking situation occurs, report the cabin situation to the captain by interphone. When it is difficult to report the cabin situation in a plain language, cabin crew must report to captain by hijack warning bell. Cabin crew prevent disturbances by reassuring passengers. Also pay attention to hijacker handling and be prepared for an emergency landing.

Aircraft	Bell Location
A330	L1, R4, All Galley
A320	L1, R3, All Galley
B737	L1, R2, All Galley
CS300	L1, L2, R2, All Galley

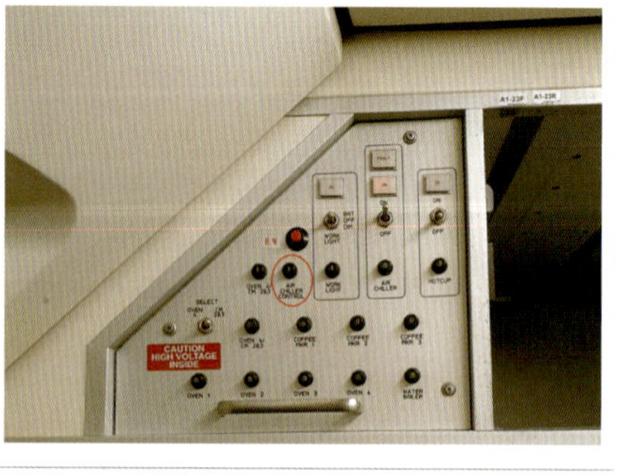

2. Cockpit Crew Procedure

- Turn on the 'Fasten Seat Belt' and the 'No Smoking' sign.
- If possible, relay the information of a hijacker to the ground.
- Consider an emergency descent when aircraft is at or above 10,000 feet.
- Attempt to make an emergency landing at the nearest/appropriate airport.

• Turn On the Seat Belt/No Smoking

• Relay the Information

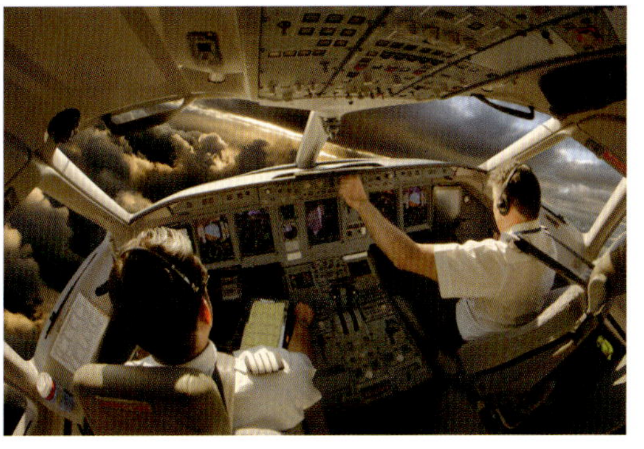

• Descend Aircraft

• Emergency Landing

Student Activity - **Team Discussion**

Read the article and answer the questions.

AirAsia flight returns to Kolkata airport after bomb scare

(source: https://economictimes.indiatimes.com)

Q1. What did the captain do after the bomb threat?

Q2. The crew's actions are not mentioned in detail. Discuss with your team members what to do if you were a cabin crew on this flight?

Q3. Find out other bomb threat cases with your team members, and share them with other classmates.

Student Activity - **Part IV Practical Evaluation**

1. Security Check

	Subject	Contents	1	2	3
Cabin Security Check	Cabin	Magazine Rack			
		Seat			
		Aisle			
		Jumpseat			
		Door			
	Lavatory	Facility			
		Compartment			
	Galley	Compartment			
		Cart			
Boarding Pass Check & Guide the Seat	Flight No.	Properly check the flight number?			
	Date	Properly check the flight date?			
	Seat	Properly guide to the passenger's seat?			

2. Unruly Passenger, Bomb Threat Handling

Unruly Passenger, Bomb Threat Handling				
Subject	Contents	1	2	3
Unruly Passenger	Take appropriate action based on the threat level?			
	Restrain and detain disruptive passenger promptly by using security equipment?			
Bomb Threat	Follow the procedures to move the explosive to the LRBL.			

Appendix

I. Terms, Definitions and Abbreviations

A

- A/C: Abbreviation for aircraft
- AED: Automatic External Defibrillator. An AED is a device about the size of a laptop computer that analyses the heart's rhythm for any abnormalities and, if necessary, directs the rescuer to deliver an electrical shock to the patients. This shock, called defibrillation, may help the heart to re-establish an effective rhythm of its own.
- AFT: Aft, back of aircraft
- ALT: Altitude
- APU: Auxiliary Power Unit
- Aileron: A small appendage to the trailing edge of the wing which controls the rolling or banking movement of the aircraft.
- Air Traffic Control (ATC): The **tower** which controls aircraft for take-offs and landings.
- Automatic Pilot: Keeps plane on a predetermined course at a desired altitude.

B

- Belly: The lower part of the aircraft fuselage or underside of the aircraft.
- Boarding/Board: The action of passengers leaving the terminal building and embarking onto the aircraft.
- Bulkhead: Solid, rigid divider used to separate portions of the aircraft cabin and/or fuselage.
- Baggage: Luggage carried on the same flight and aircraft as the passenger.

C

- C/A: Cabin Attendant

- CAPT: Captain
- CB: Circuit Breaker
- Cabin: The interior of the airplane, the portion of the fuselage lying between the cockpit and the tail section of an aircraft.
- Captain: The captain is responsible for the operation and the safety of the aircraft as well as the safety of all persons on board the aircraft during the flight. For this purpose, he/she will have final authority for the disposition of the aircraft during the time in which he/she is in command. In the event of incapacitation of the designated captain in flight , the senior qualified first officer will assume the functions of the captain.
- Configuration: The pattern of seats, cargo partitions and other items on a particular airplane or flight.
- Crew: Any person having duties on board in connection with the flying or the safety of the passengers and the aircraft.
- Cruising Speed: The speed at which an airplane may fly, the most efficient and economic speed of flight.
- CAT: Clear Air Turbulence. Turbulence which occurs in clear air with no cloud formation to give warning of its existence.
- Cockpit: Area of the aircraft fuselage which houses the flight controls, flight instruments, and flight crew (Forward or nose of the aircraft).

D

- Deadhead (D/H): To ride on a flight as a passenger in order to position for a flight which the cabin crew will be working or to return to base after a flight they have worked.
- De-icing: To remove ice, freezing rain or snow from aircraft surfaces using an alcohol solution.
- Demo: Demonstration
- Deplane: Disembarking from the aircraft.
- Destination: The ultimate stopping place of any flight; where the flight will end.
- Disembarkation: The act of leaving the aircraft after a flight.
- Drag: A retarding force which is created by the total resistance of the air to the aircraft moving through it.
- Delay: Any postponement of a flight's departure, usually due to weather or mechanical

difficulties.

- DOT: Department of Transport; governs and controls all civil aeronautics.
- Ditching: Emergency landing on water.

E

- Elevators: Control surfaces hinged on the trailing edge of the horizontal stabilizer which controls the pitch or the movement of the nose up or down.
- ELT: Emergency Locator Transmitter
- EMK: Emergency Medical Kit
- EVAC CMD: Evacuation Command
- EY: Economy Class
- En-route: Portion of the flight between take-off and landing on a specific leg of the flight.

F

- F/C: First Class
- F/O: First Officer. A licensed pilot serving in any piloting capacity other than pilot-in-command. This individual occupies the right hand seat in the cockpit.
- FWD: Forward, front of aircraft.
- FAA: U.S. Federal Aviation Agency; equivalent to the Ministry of Transport.
- Flap: An auxiliary airfoil usually hinged or pivoted to the trailing edge of the wing. Its purpose is to increase lift, or reduce speed in landing.
- Flight Plan: A listing of route, altitude and elapsed times predicted in advance of the flight and planned so as to take advantage of the most favorable winds and smoothest altitudes.
- Fleet: All aircraft belonging to a company.
- Fuselage: The main body of the aircraft. Houses the cockpit, cabin and cargo.

G

- GPU: Ground Power Unit. It is used to provide power when the engines are not running to avoid draining the ship's batteries. Unit is independent of the A/C.
- Galley: The kitchen section of an aircraft.
- Gate: Area passengers are held in within the airport terminal prior to boarding a flight.
- Gravity Force: Gravitational force. The pressure applied to an object in motion by the

Earth's gravitational pull.

H

- Hangar: A garage for aircraft.
- Headwind: A wind whose direction is meeting the aircraft head on. Will cause a reduction in the aircraft's ground speed proportional to the wind speed.
- Hold: Wait

I

- IFE: In-flight Entertainment
- Inbound: Traveling into or toward a station or destination.
- Initial: First
- Inspection: Check
- ICAO: International Civil Aviation Organization. International governing body responsible for determining and maintaining standards in international publication, etc.
- IATA: International Air Transport Association
- ILS: Instrument Landing System. Navigational aid used to aid pilot in the approach to landing at an airport.

J

- Jumpseat: Seat designed solely for the use of cabin crew or, in case of the cockpit jumpseat, authorized personnel only.

K

- Knots: Speed measurement. Divide kilometers per hour by 1.853 to get knots.
  - · 1km/h = 0.54 knots   100 kmph = 54 knots
  - · 1 knot = 1.853 km/h   100 knots = 185.3 kmph

L

- LRBL: Least Risk Bomb Location
- LAV: Lavatory
- Load Sheet: Document listing all goods, Pax, etc. to be carried onboard a flight as well

as weights and crew members.

- Leading Edge: Edge of a control surface which is the most forward or lead the surface through the air.

M

- MEL: Minimum Equipment List. List of equipment which must be serviceable and onboard an aircraft in order to fly.

N

- Nose: The most forward portion of the aircraft fuselage.

O

- Outbound: Traveling away from a station or point.

P

- PAX: Passenger
- PBE: Protective Breathing Equipment
- PSU: Passenger Service Unit. Console containing air vents, reading lights, and oxygen outlet, etc.
- PTT: Push To Talk
- PA: Public Address System
- Pallet: Portable platform used to store and transport cargo onboard the aircraft.
- PIC: Pilot in Command. Captain
- Pre-Flight: Prior to departure.
- P/M: Passenger Manifest. It contains listing of passenger names and other additional information. To be completed for each flight with copies on board and at departure station.
- Pitch: The action which occurs when the nose of the plane moves up and down.

R

- RTO: Rejected Take-Off
- Ramp: Area at an airport designed for the movement and parking of aircraft.
- Runway: Area of an airport designed for the take-off and landing movements of aircraft.

Active runway defines the runway which, due to wind direction, is being used when two or more runways exist.

- Roll: Movement of the A/C caused by the ailerons.
- Rudder: Moveable control surface attached to the vertical stabilizer. Controls the movement of the A/C. Also termed YAW.

S

- Stabilizer: Section of the tail which stabilizes aircraft in flight.

T

- Taxi: Movement of the aircraft on the ground when the aircraft is operating under its own power.
- Tailwind: Wind direction that is paralleling the aircraft's heading, or blowing in the same direction that the aircraft is flying in.
- Tail: The section of the A/C which is most rearward. Consists of horizontal stabilizer, vertical stabilizer, elevator and rudder.
- Taxiway: Area of the airport designed for the movement and positioning of A/C for take-off and boarding/deplaning.
- Turbulence: Rough air caused by winds from hot and cold air masses meeting.
- Thrust: The force resulting from the hot exhaust gases from the jet engines which push the plane forward.

U

- UM: Unaccompanied Minor

Y

- YAW: Movement of the A/C controlled by the rudder.

II. Phonetic Alphabet

To ensure a clear and effective communication in the aviation business, the letters of the alphabet are referred to as follows:

A	ALPHA	B	BRAVO	C	CHARLIE
D	DELTA	E	ECHO	F	FOXTROT
G	GOLF	H	HOTEL	I	INDIA
J	JULIET	K	KILO	L	LIMA
M	MIKE	N	NOVEMBER	O	OSCAR
P	PAPA	Q	QUEBEC	R	ROMEO
S	SIERRA	T	TANGO	U	UNIFORM
V	VICTORY	W	WHISKEY	X	X-RAY
Y	YANKEE	Z	ZULU		

III. Time Zone

There are 24 hours in a day and 24 time zones. Time zones extend from the North Pole to the South Pole. An area's time zone is determined by the area's distance east or west of Greenwich, England. Greenwich Mean Time (GMT) is the basis of Standard Time Zone throughout most of the world. Coordinated Universal Time (UTC) is the basis for civil time today. This 24-hour time standard is kept using highly precise atomic clocks combined with the Earth's rotation. UTC is the time standard commonly used across the world. The world's timing centers have agreed to keep their time scales closely synchronized–or coordinated–therefore the name Coordinated Universal Time. Greenwich Mean Time (GMT) is often interchanged or confused with Coordinated Universal Time (UTC). But GMT is a time zone and UTC is a time standard. Standard Time is defined as the official civil time for any given region. Daylight Savings Time is one hour later than the Standard Time. Neither UTC nor GMT ever change for Daylight Saving Time (DST). However, some of the countries that use GMT switch to different time zones during their DST period. For example, the United Kingdom is not on GMT all year, it uses British Summer Time (BST), which is one hour ahead of GMT, during the summer months. The **official watch** of Korean Air and Asiana Airline are set on Korean Standard Time (KST; UTC +9)

IV. 24-Hour Clock

The 24-hour clock is used to precisely represent the time of the day. A 24-hour clock time eliminates the necessity of including AM or PM in a time. Airlines, the military, and many foreign countries use the 24-hour clock.

e.g. 9:15 AM = 09:15   5:00 PM = 17:00

V. IATA 3-Letter Codes

Each city destination worldwide has been assigned and is identified by a three-letter city code. Each airport also has a three-letter airport code. Sometimes the city code and the airport code are the same. Cities with more than one airport have a separate and different code for each airport. Airport codes are derived from the first three letters in the city's name, a combination of three letters in the city's name, a combination of three letters in the city's and state's name or a combination of three letters in the airport's name. Some airport codes are derived from unidentified sources. For example, New York City code is NYC, but New York's three main airports are LaGuardia (LGA), Kennedy (JFK), and Newark (EWR).

Official Name of Airport and Three Letter Code

1. Oceania Region STN Code

CODE	NAME	CITY CODE	CITY	COUNTRY
AKL	Auckland	AKL	Auckland	New Zealand
BNE	Brisbane	BNE	Brisbane	Australia
CHC	Christchurch	CHC	Christchurch	New Zealand
SYD	Sydney	SYD	Sydney	Australia

MEL	Melbourne	MEL	Melbourne	Australia
NAN	Nadi	NAN	Nadi	Fiji
SPN	Saipan	SPN	Saipan	U.S.A
GUM	Guam	GUM	Guam	U.S.A

2. Japan Region STN Code

CODE	NAME	CITY CODE	CITY	COUNTRY
AOJ	Aomori	AOJ	Aomori	Japan
AXT	Akita	AXT	Akita	Japan
CTS	New Chitose	SPK	Sapporo	Japan
FUK	Fukuoka	FUK	Fukuoka	Japan
KIJ	Niigata	KIJ	Niigata	Japan
KIX	Kansai	OSA	Osaka	Japan
ITM	Itami	OSA	Osaka	Japan
KOJ	Kagoshima	KOJ	Kagoshima	Japan
NGO	Chubu Central	NGO	Nagoya	Japan
NRT	Narita	TYO	Tokyo	Japan
HND	Haneda	TYO	Tokyo	Japan
OIT	Oita	OIT	Oita	Japan
OKJ	Okayama	OKJ	Okayama	Japan
OKA	Naha	OKA	Okinawa	Japan
SDJ	Sendai	SDJ	Sendai	Japan
TOY	Toyama	TOY	Toyama	Japan
HIJ	Hiroshima	HIJ	Hiroshima	Japan
KKJ	Kita Kyushu	KKJ	Kita Kyushu	Japan
NGS	Nagasaki	NGS	Nagasaki	Japan

3. Asia STN Code

CODE	NAME	CITY CODE	CITY	COUNTRY
BKK	Suvarnabhumi	BKK	Bangkok	Thailand
BOM	Chhatrapati Shivaji	BOM	Mumbai	India
CGK	Soekarno-Hatta	JKT	Jakarta	Indonesia
KUL	Kuala Lumpur	KUL	Kuala Lumpur	Malaysia

MNL	Ninoy Aquino	MNL	Manila	Philippines
SGN	Tan Son Nhat	SGN	Ho Chi Minh City	Vietnam
SIN	Singapore Changi	SIN	Singapore	Singapore
ULN	Chinggis Khaan	ULN	Ulaan Baatar	Mongolia
MFM	Macau	MFM	Macau	Macau
PEN	Penang	PEN	Penang	Malaysia
DEL	Indira Gandhi	DEL	New Delhi	India
DPS	Ngurah Rai	DPS	Denpasar (Bali)	Indonesia
HAN	Noi Bai	HAN	Hanoi	Vietnam
HKT	Phuket	HKT	Phuket	Thailand
TPE	Taiwan Taoyuan	TPE	Taipei	Taiwan

4. China STN Code

CODE	NAME	CITY CODE	CITY	COUNTRY
TNA	Jinan Yaoqiang	TNA	Jinan	China
SYX	Sanya Phoenix	SYX	Sanya	China
HKG	Hong Kong	HKG	Hong Kong	China
PEK	Beijing Capital	BJS	Beijing	China
SHA	Shanghai Hongqiao	SHA	Shanghai	China
PVG	Shanghai Pudong	SHA	Shanghai	China
SHE	Shenyang Taoxian	SHE	Shenyang	China
TAO	Qingdao Liuting	TAO	Qingdao	China
YNT	Yantai Laishan	YNT	Yantai	China
XMN	Xiamen Gaoqi	XMN	Xiamen	China
WUH	Wuhan Tianhe	WUH	Wuhan	China
KMG	Kunming Changshui	KMG	Kunming	China
CAN	Guangzhou Baiyun	CAN	Guangzhou	China
TSN	Tianjin Binhai	TSN	Tianjin	China

5. Europe Region STN Code

CODE	NAME	CITY CODE	CITY	COUNTRY
CDG	Charles de Gaulle	PAR	Paris	France
FCO	Fiumicino	ROM	Rome	Italy

FRA	Frankfurt	FRA	Frankfurt	Germany
LHR	Heathrow	LON	London	U.K.
SVO	Sheremetyevo	MOW	Moscow	Rusia
VVO	Vladivostok	VVO	Vladivostok	Rusia
ZRH	Kloten	ZRH	Zurich	Switzerland
BRU	Brussels	BRU	Brussels	Belgium
CPH	Copenhagen	CPH	Copenhagen	Denmark
MXP	Malpensa	MIL	Milan	Italy
TAS	Tashkent	TAS	Tashkent	Uzbekistan
ALA	Almaty	ALA	Almaty	Kazakhstan
DUB	Dublin	DUB	Dublin	Ireland
IST	Istanbul	IST	Istanbul	Turkey
LGW	Gatwick	LON	London	U.K
LIS	Lisbon	LIS	Lisbon	Portugal
LUX	Luxembourg	LUX	Luxembourg	Luxembourg
MAD	Madrid–Barajas	MAD	Madrid	Spain
ORY	Orly	PAR	Paris	France
OSL	Oslo	OSL	Oslo	Norway
AMS	Schiphol	AMS	Amsterdam	Netherlands
ARN	Stockholm-Arlanda	STO	Stockholm	Sweden
TXL	Berlin Tegel	BER	Berlin	Germany
VIE	Vienna	VIE	Vienna	Austria

6. Africa/Middle East STN Code

CODE	NAME	CITY CODE	CITY	COUNTRY
BAH	Bahrain	BAH	Bahrain	Bahrain
CAI	Cairo	CAI	Cairo	Egypt
DHA	Dhahran	DHA	Dhahran	Saudi Arabia
DXB	Dubai	DXB	Dubai	U.A.E
JED	King Abdulaziz	JED	Jeddah	Saudi Arabia
TLV	Ben Gurion	TLV	Tel Aviv	Israel
THR	Mehrabad	THR	Tehran	Iran
TIP	Tripoli	TIP	Tripoli	Libya

7. America STN Code

CODE	NAME	CITY CODE	CITY	COUNTRY
ANC	Ted Stevens Anchorage	ANC	Anchorage	U.S.A
ATL	Hartsfield-Jackson Atlanta	ATL	Atlanta	U.S.A
BOS	Logan	BOS	Boston	U.S.A
DEN	Denver	DEN	Denver	U.S.A
DFW	Dallas/Fort Worth	DAL	Dallas	U.S.A
EWR	Newark	NYC	Newark/New York	U.S.A
HNL	Honolulu	HNL	Honolulu	U.S.A
IAD	Dulles	WAS	Washington, D.C.	U.S.A
JFK	John F. Kennedy	NYC	New York	U.S.A
LAS	McCarran	LAS	Las Vegas	U.S.A
LAX	Los Angeles	LAX	Los Angeles	U.S.A
ORD	O'Hare	CHI	Chicago	U.S.A
ORL	Orlando	ORL	Orlando	U.S.A
PHL	Philadelphia	PHL	Philadelphia	U.S.A
SFO	San Francisco	SFO	San Francisco	U.S.A
YVR	Vancouver	YVR	Vancouver	Canada
YYZ	Lester B. Pearson	YYZ	Toronto	Canada
GRU	Guarulhos	SAO	Sao Paulo	Brazil
DTW	Detroit Metropolitan	DTT	Detroit	U.S.A
LGA	LaGuardia	NYC	New York	U.S.A
MIA	Miami	MIA	Miami	U.S.A
MSP	Minneapolis - St Paul	MSP	Minneapolis	U.S.A
SEA	Tacoma	SEA	Seattle	U.S.A
EZE	Ministro Pistarini	BUE	Buenos Aires	Argentina
GIG	Galeao	RIO	Rio de Janeiro	Brazil
MEX	Mexico City	MEX	Mexico City	Mexico
SCL	Santiago	SCL	Santiago	Chille

Reference

- Korean Air. Cabin Operations Manual
- Emirates. Aircraft Familiarizations
- IATA. Airline Cabin Crew Training 3rd edition
- Transport Canada. Brace for Impact Positions for all Aircraft Occupants
- http://www.Boeing.com
- http://www.Airbus.com
- https://www.bombardier.com/en/home.html
- https://embraer.com/global/en
- https://www.skybrary.aero/index.php/Unruly_Passengers